TEST CONSTRUCTION

DATE DUE

JAN - 6 2006

TEST CONSTRUCTION

Development and Interpretation
of Achievement Tests

DOROTHY ADKINS WOOD
University of North Carolina

Charles E. Merrill Publishing Co.
Columbus, Ohio
A Bell and Howell Company

Library of Congress Catalog Card Number:
60-13160

10 11 12 13 14 15-76 75 74 73 72 71 70 69 68

Printed in the United States of America

Preface

This book is addressed to both experienced and prospective teachers at all educational levels, as well as to inexperienced testers in fields other than education. Perhaps its principal purpose is to expedite the transition from theory to practice, or to help to erase the cultural lag in the development and widespread use of psychological testing techniques drawn from an integrated body of subject matter that can be taught. The treatment of statistical methods useful in dealing with test scores is confined to minimum essentials, with no effort having been made to present derivations or the more advanced concepts and techniques. No prerequisite knowledge of statistics is assumed.

Universities will find the book appropriate for use as a supplementary textbook for such courses as educational psychology, educational or psychological measurement, personnel administration, or test construction per se. The material could be covered in from two to four, or even more, weeks, depending upon the amount of supplementary reading and laboratory practice in test development that the instructor wished to assign.

The busy teacher already engaged in evaluating student achievement should find a few hours with this book to be a worthwhile investment. A teacher who has been using unduly time-consuming methods in constructing and scoring tests will find a number of helpful suggestions for conserving time as well as for improving his teaching and his evaluation of student performance.

Although the book deals most directly with educational achievement testing, many of the principles and procedures described are applicable to the development of aptitude tests and to the use of achievement tests in other settings, as, for example, in personnel selection. Thus, persons engaged in testing applicants for industrial and government employment will find this brief treatment helpful, particularly in providing basic training for new personnel to be employed in testing programs.

To conserve reading time, the author has omitted citations of particular sources of many ideas, some of which would have been impossible to trace in any case. She has felt free to re-use some of the concepts treated earlier in a book on *Construction and Analysis of Achievement Tests,* of which she was senior author while employed by the United States Civil Service Commission and which is now out of print. Thus, she acknowledges her debt to her collaborators in that earlier venture: Ernest S. Primoff, Harold L. McAdoo, Claude F. Bridges, and Bertram Forer.

The author has benefitted so greatly from John M. Stalnaker's chapter on "The Essay Type of Examination" in *Educational Measurement* (edited by E. F. Lindquist and published by the American Council on Education in 1951) that she expresses her special gratitude to him.

She also states here her deep appreciation to Max D. Engelhart, Director, Department of Examinations, The Chicago City Junior College, for his unusual generosity in permitting her to draw illustrative materials freely and extensively from examinations developed under his direction. One set of his items, which was previously published in *Educational and Psychological Measurement,* was included with the permission of G. Frederic Kuder, the editor of the journal.

Two charts, illustrating examination plans, have been reproduced from *Comprehensive Examinations in a Program of General Education,* by Paul L. Dressel (ed.), with the permission of The Michigan State University Press. A computing chart, useful in the analysis of individual test items, has been adapted, by permission, from one in Charles I. Mosier and John V. McQuitty's "Methods of Item Validation and Abacs for Item-Test Correlation and Critical Ratio of Upper-Lower Difference," *Psychometrika,* V, No. 1 (March 1940), pp. 57–65.

Although a large number of references might have been cited in a bibliography, the alternative of presenting a small number of selected titles at the end of the book seemed more appropriate to the author's purposes. Books on principles of constructing and interpreting tests are included, as well as books on elementary statistics. Some of the listed books, of course, contain numerous additional references that will be useful to the reader who wishes to delve further into various aspects of the testing field.

Chapel Hill, North Carolina   D. A. W.
November, 1959

Contents

Chapter 1

Introduction

The testing movement has made rapid strides indeed in the last thirty years. The use of standardized tests as both diagnostic and predictive devices in elementary and secondary schools has increased immensely. Procedures used for selecting government employees ordinarily include tests, and the armed services tailor-make hundreds of different tests to ensure the most appropriate placement of men. Industry, too, in the selection and placement of employees has come to rely heavily upon various types of measuring devices.

In schools, standardized tests are far less common than those devised by the teacher himself. These teacher-made tests, upon which students' marks are customarily based, often reveal serious shortcomings. Their faults may arise from such causes as inadequate consideration by the teacher of the objectives of instruction, technical defects in construction, the teacher's failure to appreciate those factors that make scores undependable, or his inability to apply even rudimentary statistical treatment to test scores. This problem exists in spite of the fact that the school teacher has ordinarily been required to study educational psychology, which includes testing as one of its topics. Some teachers may also have had a separate course in tests and measurements. For all their value, such special courses are usually not geared to producing competence in test construction but more often treat commercially available tests that may prove valuable in an educational setting. Thus the teacher often completes his educational program with little understanding of testing principles and practices.

Strangely enough, an even more significant lag in the application of basic principles of psychological measurement is evident in our colleges and universities. This may be attributed, at least in part, to the fact that teachers at this level have usually not been subjected to any formal training at all in educational or psychological measurement. In any case, for whatever reasons, the appraisal of educational achievement in colleges and universities has a horse-and-buggy look. Discussions at college faculty meetings bearing on such matters as marking systems reveal not merely an apathetic attitude toward the problems concerned but often gross misconceptions.

This book represents an attempt to improve educational examining by making available to teachers and prospective teachers a brief, straightforward, and understandable treatment of measurement techniques. The plan is to present general measurement principles, more specific rules for test construction, and statistical techniques that can be applied by the reader to any subject-matter field. No effort has been made to include separate chapters dealing with the applications of these principles and techniques to each of a large number of subject-matter fields. For the most part, illustrative test material introduced in the course of the book will be based upon the content of the book itself rather than upon different subject-matter areas which would be unequally familiar to readers. The specialist in English history, for example, would have difficulty understanding illustrative test items based on physics or a foreign language. In the appendices, however, approximately one hundred objective test items are presented from various subject-matter areas. These will illustrate the different types of questions that can be posed as well as the flexibility of the multiple-choice form of item.

What does a raw score of 62 on an hour quiz in a history course mean? How should such a number be translated into a letter grade? How should this grade be averaged with numbers achieved on other tests? How are the weights at which different test scores are combined to be determined? What is the relationship of scores on one test to scores on another test? When a test is needed that is equivalent to one previously given, how can the comparability of the two tests be assured? Is the true-false form likely to be as good as the multiple-choice? Can these or other objective tests be used if a teacher is interested in appraising more than the acquisition of factual knowledge? When is it necessary and when useless to apply "correction for guessing"? How can the framing and scoring of essay tests be improved? What are the arguments against the use of optional items? How can the scoring of objective tests be expedited? What are the basic principles for constructing good test items? How can one determine the value of individual items? How can errors in the scoring be detected before final scores are assigned? What is the impact of a testing program upon the curriculum? To what extent can tests be used not merely as measuring devices but, perhaps more important, as teaching devices? To these and related questions this book is addressed.

Chapter 2

The General Nature of Educational Achievement Tests

INDIVIDUAL DIFFERENCES

If all students enrolled in a course of instruction had identical aptitudes, interests, and motivation and if they had been subjected to the same environmental forces, no differences among them would be revealed either at the beginning or at the end of the course. The very nature of the organization of our educational system, however, ensures that students will differ in relevant characteristics both before and after exposure to particular segments of subject matter. If individuals did not vary, the field of testing would never have developed. Faced with differences in abilities, however, educators and psychologists became interested in how to measure them and in what types of recommendations could reasonably be made upon the basis of these measurements.

TESTS AS PREDICTORS

The kinds of decisions that arise from a consideration of test results are, in the last analysis, in the nature of *predictions*. If these predictions are not substantiated by later developments to an extent greater than chance would warrant one to expect, then, for one reason or another, the tests have failed to achieve their purposes.

Achievement and Aptitude Tests as Predictors

This element of prediction may not be so evident in the case of *academic achievement* tests as in the case of *academic aptitude* tests or of those used for selecting or placing employees. Although the distinction between aptitude and achievement tests is by no means as definite as has often been supposed, the emphasis in the case of aptitude tests has been more on potential abilities, as for future learning or job performance, and less upon the current abilities or specific knowledge now evidenced by the subject. Thus when one of the several kinds of tests that have gone under the name of "general intelligence" tests is given to applicants for college admission, the purpose is to predict how well they will do in college. Such a test would commonly be classified as an aptitude test. On the other hand, a teacher who gives a final examination in economics thinks of his purpose as that of testing the students' present mastery of the content of the course. This test is referred to as an achievement test. Knowledge of the subject matter today, however, can be of little consequence unless there is some residue tomorrow. Basically, then, the teacher must be interested in making a prediction from today's test score as to the future behavior of the student. This is true no matter how obscure and tenuous the prediction may be in last-minute scurrying to report grades to some central administrative office. As the student's transcript accompanies him in his postgraduate years, when he seeks admission to a curriculum for further training or an employment opportunity, the record of his over-all academic achievement is in some way being used to make predictions as to his likelihood of success in new undertakings.

Counseling as Prediction

When either aptitude or achievement tests are used in educational and vocational counseling, the counselor is assisting the student in *making predictions*. These predictions may relate to the academic subjects in which the student will probably do best and poorest with equal expenditures of effort or to the fields of work in which he is most likely to achieve success. Armed with scores on a number of aptitude tests, perhaps an interest inventory, and one or more multiple-scored personality question-naires, together with records of previous scholastic attainments and im-pressions gleaned from interviews, the counselor summarizes his impres-sions in one or more predictions. Whether he combines the evidence from the different sources by strictly statistical means or by a more impres-sionistic method of weighting variables, he is still making predictions.

Diagnosis as Prediction

A purpose of testing that is sometimes differentiated from prediction is *diagnosis*. Here the emphasis is upon the patterning of relative strengths and weaknesses or of peaks and gaps in abilities. A test to be used in this way must be so arranged as to provide separate scores on the specific areas in which diagnostic interest centers. The use of tests for diagnostic purposes typically occurs in an educational setting, where the immediate aim is to spot areas in which additional instruction needs to be given or in which teaching methods may need to be altered. Such a goal, while seem-ingly different from prediction, is not really inconsistent with the view that prediction is the ultimate aim of testing. From relative strengths and weaknesses in test performance, a prediction is made as to the behavior that can be expected to ensue unless changes are made.

TESTS AS TEACHING AIDS

Motivating the Student

So far our discussion has been concerned principally with the use of tests as *measuring devices*. This use is paramount in employee-selection testing and in much educational testing. Another very significant use of tests in the classroom, one that warrants further extension, is as a *direct aid in motivation and thus in teaching*. The most obvious aspect of this use of testing is that students who know they are to be tested will often do more studying and hence learn more than would otherwise be the case. Cramming merely for the purpose of passing a test, with no intent to re-member beyond it, is poor practice. Nevertheless, even this approach to learning undoubtedly results in more knowledge than would no studying at all. In addition, although the tests may be poor, the student's regular preparation for periodic tests is often a positive motivating force.

Teaching While Testing

A second and perhaps more fruitful way to use tests for instructional purposes is to ensure that learning takes place either at the very time the test is given or very soon thereafter. A teacher who fails to take advantage of this method of teaching is ignoring one of the most fruitful teaching devices. Too often, a test is given, perhaps in essay form, and returned to students several days or weeks later, with numerical marks assigned to each question but without any clear and detailed presentation of what would constitute an adequate or a superior response to the question. Under such a system, the student has lost his motivation by the time he gets some vague impression from the teacher of the answers that were expected of him. Objective tests are more easily scored and returned to students before much time has elapsed. They also enable the student to know more exactly what answer was intended for each question. Even when objective tests are used, however, teachers frequently delay having them scored and allow too little time for discussion. They often fail to apply some simple statistical techniques which would help them to spot the questions that need most discussion, or they are so eager to proceed to new topics that they resist adequate discussion of the questions. Thus they fail to take advantage of the immediate and powerful incentive to learning that is provided by a prompt knowledge of progress.

With appropriate planning, tests can be scored either while they are being taken or toward the end of the class period. For example, a test that ordinarily requires a fifty-minute period could be divided into two parts, a half of each of two periods to be devoted to taking the test and the latter half to having the students score it. This suggestion, of course, implies that the test in question is of the objective type. The scoring itself would require very little time, so that there would be an opportunity for discussion. When the student learns immediately which items he has had trouble with and the correct responses, he is much more likely to correct his misconceptions than if he must wait several days or perhaps never be informed of his specific errors.

Special Teaching Devices

Still better would be some practical device that immediately informs the student of the correct answer to each question before he proceeds to the next. One device for accomplishing this purpose was developed by Dr.

S. L. Pressey in the late 1920's. Used with multiple-choice questions, his cash-register-like machine had numbered buttons one of which was to be pushed to indicate the student's first choice of an answer to the question whose number appeared in a window of the machine. If his choice was incorrect, the question number remained the same and he punched another button, until he selected the correct answer. When he had completed all of the items, he had been informed of the correct answer to each. His score, consisting of the total number of attempts he required to reach the correct answers for all the questions, automatically appeared on the machine.

Another more recent development along somewhat the same lines is the teaching machine on which Dr. B. F. Skinner and his colleagues are currently at work. Here the curricular material is broken down into small teaching units which can be presented on the face of a machine. As the subject-matter material proceeds through the machine, the learner is actively making responses that automatically demonstrate his mastery of the material, and he does not finish with a particular unit of instruction until he has achieved the requisite degree of mastery. This machine is another illustration of the way in which testing, with immediate indication of progress, can be used to facilitate learning. Skinner's device is still in the developmental stages and, as currently envisaged, will require extensive work in the preparation of curricular materials for use with the machine. A number of other persons are working on other teaching and testing developments that seem likely to require less work and little special equipment. These various ways in which tests can be used as instructional devices should be suggestive to teachers.

Adjustment of Teaching to Student Abilities

Another way in which tests may have an impact on teaching is by separating students, for instructional purposes, into groups that are relatively homogeneous in abilities. Such subdivision of classes is practical only in the case of a large group of students who are to be taught the same subject matter in smaller groups, as, for example, in freshman English or mathematics. In such circumstances, tests of relevant aptitudes can be of great help in grouping the students so that both the content and the teaching methods can be made appropriate to the abilities of the class.

As a matter of fact, in a good educational system, the aptitudes and previous achievements of each individual student are a matter of continuous record, readily available to a teacher so that student assignments and the goals set for them can be adjusted in the light of their abilities. Even when subdivision of classes into groups homogeneous in ability is not feasible, the teacher may well find a record of the scores of each of the students on pertinent aptitudes to be advantageous. Moreover, some students often know more about a particular subject at the beginning of a course than others will at the end. A test on the content of a course given at its beginning may thus be quite revealing. Such a test might be an equivalent form of a typical final examination in the course.

In any case, many schools and universities now have some sort of aptitude examination program. Records on such tests as are given, although they may not be routinely available to instructors, would undoubtedly be accessible upon request. Such test data, as for example on tests of verbal abilities, quantitative abilities, English, and mathematics, will assist the teacher in adjusting to the individual students whose behavior he is attempting to modify.

The purpose of this book is to assist teachers in making better use of tests both as measuring devices and as aids in the instructional process. Our concern is primarily with tests in the cognitive realm. Although there are many interesting developments in the testing of interests, attitudes, and other personality characteristics, these are specialized fields that would require separate handling and in which the teacher is not ordinarily expected to make direct original contributions. Hence our treatment will be concerned principally with the development and use of academic achievement tests, with which every teacher must be familiar.

Chapter 3

Principles of
Psychological Measurement

THE MEANING OF MEASUREMENT

In the strictest concept of measurement, some kind of scale along which equal units can be indicated and on which the position zero corresponds to "just nothing" of whatever is being measured is regarded as a necessity. Thus it is with a yardstick. The user has confidence that one inch anywhere along the scale is exactly equal for all practical purposes to an inch arbitrarily chosen along any other point of the scale. Moreover, zero inches has for him rational significance as corresponding to the absence of any length whatever. With such a measuring instrument, one length can meaningfully be expressed as a multiple of another length. Thus it makes sense to say that a stick ten inches long has twice the length of a stick five inches long.

Necessary conditions for such a statement are that the units be equal and that the origin or zero point on the scale have some rational meaning corresponding to the "nothingness" of physical reality. With such a scale, one can also justifiably express one gain or increment as a multiple of another. Thus a gain of eight points from 40 to 48 is four times the gain of two points from 21 to 23. To make such a statement requires that the units be equal but not necessarily that the zero point be meaningful.

The fact may as well be faced that the vast majority of educational and psychological tests meets neither of the foregoing conditions. A score of zero on an educational achievement test, for example, rarely corresponds to "just no knowledge." Moreover, in the typical achievement test, a gain of one score point comes from answering correctly one additional item. Since only in exceptional cases, as in certain types of speed of performance tests, are the items completely equivalent and thus interchangeable, the score units are not equal in the sense that analogy to physical measurement would require. Hence achievement tests typically have neither equal units nor anything other than an arbitrary zero point. While the presence of these two conditions of physical measurement would be a source of some comfort and convenience, their absence by no means leads to the conclusion that no worthwhile results can accrue from psychological measurement. The teacher does not need to be able to make the statement that one student's test performance is a particular multiple of the performance of another in order to make useful predictions about their relative future behavior or to use tests effectively as instructional tools. Although counting the number of items passed or awarding differential scoring values to different test performances yields scores in quantitative terms, many of the advantages of this practice are fortunately not dependent upon the exact equivalence of the units. In actuality, test scores are often treated as though the unequal units were equal in applications of certain familiar statistical methods. Also available are statistical tools that do not imply equal units but only the ability to establish qualitative differences among different performances or to place them in rank order.

THE CONCEPT OF TEST RELIABILITY

Score differences should be mainly due to factors other than chance. This lack of dependence upon chance variation is the essence of the concept of *test reliability*. There are three principal sources of chance variation in test scores that should be minimized or avoided.

Scoring Unreliability

First is *scorer unreliability*. A test score may be unreliable in the sense that the score depends to too great an extent upon the particular person who does the scoring. This factor is often quite significant in the case of essay tests but can be reduced to no importance in the case of objective tests. For essay tests, scorer inconsistencies may be investigated by comparing scores assigned by the same scorer to the same test at different times. Even a single scorer may assign quite markedly different scores to the same paper after a lapse of time. Scorer unreliability will be even more evident when the scores assigned by two different but presumably equally competent persons are inspected.

In either case, to make such comparisons most conveniently and in summary form requires the use of some index of the relationship between two sets of scores. If high scores in one set are associated with high scores in the other and low scores in the two sets likewise accompany each other, the relationship is *positive*. When low scores in one group go with high scores in the other, the relationship is *negative*. One might use a Pearson product-moment correlation coefficient, r, if the number of cases exceeds twenty-five or thirty. Or he might use some simpler method, such as a rank-difference correlation coefficient, if the number of cases is very small.[1] These indices vary between -1.00 for a perfect negative relationship to $+1.00$ for a perfect positive relationship.

When the scoring of a test is completely objective, to the extent that any clerk provided with a scoring key can perform the scoring, the matter of scorer unreliability is of no concern. For this reason, among others, many persons have come to prefer objective tests to essay tests. Nonetheless, because the latter are still widely used, especially for small classes, methods for reducing their scorer unreliability will be described briefly in chapter 10, which deals with essay tests.

Content Unreliability

A second source of unreliability in tests arises from *poor sampling of content*. In the limited time available for a test, only a fraction of the content that might be included can be covered. Thus one might envisage a file of several thousand possible items that could legitimately be used in a particular test. Yet it must be confined to perhaps one hundred items.

[1]The concept of correlation is discussed more fully in chapter 8.

These, then, can be regarded as a sampling from the reservoir of conceivably available items.

The sample may be poor in the sense that it is too small, so that the resulting scores will depend too much upon the accidental inclusion of certain items and exclusion of others. Even though the sample is large, it may fail to be representative, so that certain areas of subject matter may be overemphasized and others neglected. In either case, the score of a student will depend too much upon the particular sampling of items. He might conceivably have received quite a different score on another test.

This type of unreliability again is more likely to afflict essay tests because by their very nature they can contain only a limited number of questions. Sampling unreliability may also affect objective tests, however, especially if the teacher finds it easier to develop items in some areas than in others or if he hastily assembles items from an unrepresentative pool of test materials. Poor sampling of content and abilities can readily be investigated by comparing the scores for two sets of items drawn to the same test specifications. Again, such a comparison can be made immediately by some type of correlation coefficient.

With some experience and awareness of content sampling as a possible source of unreliability, the teacher who follows certain precautions in the development and selection of test materials and who uses tests of sufficient length need not investigate the content reliability of every test to be used. He should learn from experience, however, the length of test and other precautions that need to be observed in order to be reasonably confident that poor sampling is not leading to basic errors in the scores assigned.

Temporal Unreliability

A third source of unreliability in test scores may be referred to as *temporal instability of performance*. This encompasses a variety of possible factors that might lead a student to get different scores on a test if he were to take it at different times. If test scores are to be useful for predictions, they must not vary appreciably over relatively short intervals of time within which it can be assumed that no basically significant changes have occurred in the individuals' abilities.

Theoretically, in order to investigate this possible source of unreliability, one would compare the scores of a group of subjects on one administration of the test with their scores on a second administration of the same test. In practice, such a comparison may be complicated by the fact that some students will simply remember the responses they made the first time and repeat these answers the second time without responding afresh to each item. Moreover, some students will remember better than others. This fact is perhaps more troublesome in the case of tests in which speed is relatively important. One might argue that sufficient time between the two administrations of the test should be allowed to negate the memory factor. If this is done, however, the possibility exists that significant changes in the basic abilities being tested have occurred. Such changes, if present, would lead to an appearance of unreliability. Yet, if they have occurred and if the test is appropriately testing these abilities, the test scores should of course reflect the changes. Fortunately, however, temporal unreliability is usually not the sole concern. Thus a study of reliability can be designed in such a way that all three of the major sources of error will be revealed if they are operating.

Measures of Various Kinds of Reliability

Consider, for example, two presumably equivalent forms of a test, designated as A and B. Such forms should have different items, and each identifiable area of subject matter should be sampled by the same number of items of presumably equal difficulty. Assume two scorers, designated as I and II, and two possible times for administering the test, separated by an interval, to be designated as 1 and 2.

Now different correlation coefficients may be thought of as possible indicators of reliability. The correlation of form A, rated by rater I and administered at time 1, with form A, rated by rater II and administered at time 1, tells us primarily about *scorer* reliability. The correlation of form A, rated by rater I and administered at time 1, with form B, rated by rater I and administered at time 1, tells us primarily about *content* reliability. The correlation between AI1 and AI2 gives us some notion of the *temporal* stability of the performance being evaluated. The reader can proceed to form various combinations for himself and determine what sources of unreliability might show up. Since ordinarily the most useful measure would be capable of being affected by all three sources, clearly the best procedure would be to correlate, say, AI1 with BII2 (or some equivalent combinations, such as AII2 with BI1).

If the scoring is objective as, for example, in a multiple-choice test, concern with scorer reliability is no longer present. In this case, reliability can be appropriately investigated by correlating one form administered at one time with another form given later.

Such an approach requires that two forms of a test be administered at different times or that one form be split into two comparable halves to be administered at different times. This method does not always seem feasible, although it is perhaps possible if appropriate plans are made. If a test is split into two parts, each half as long as the total test, then the reliability of the test in its original length can be estimated by substituting the correlation coefficient between the two halves of the test for the value r in the following formula (which is a special case of a formula known as the Spearman-Brown prophecy formula):

$$R = \frac{2r}{1+r}$$

In the foregoing formula, R stands for the estimated reliability of the total test. By the nature of the mathematical function involved, the estimated reliability of the total test will always be greater than the reliability of half of the test. This does not mean that a long test is always more reliable than a short test. But, within reasonable time limits, such that fatigue and boredom have no appreciable effect, adding comparable (equally good) items to a test may be expected to increase its reliability. The general rule is that, within limits, the longer a test, the more likely it is to have an acceptable degree of reliability.

If splitting a test into two parts to be administered at different times is not feasible, a method of estimating the reliability of a test in its entirety from a single administration can be used for a power test (that is, if speed of performance does not contribute significantly to scores on the test). Perhaps the best-known method of this type is to apply separate scoring keys to the odd-numbered items and the even-numbered items. Then the two resulting scores are correlated and the resulting coefficient is inserted as r in the prophecy formula above, to yield an estimate of the reliability of the total test. Although this method is very frequently used, it has the chief drawback that any temporal instability cannot be reflected. In addition to the split-half or odd-even approach to estimating reliability from a single administration of a test, other methods, perhaps notably the Kuder-Richardson approaches, are also available.[2]

---

[2]See, e.g., E. F. Lindquist, ed., *Educational Measurement* (Washington, D. C.: American Council on Educaiton. 1951), pp. 586–94.

None of these methods of estimating reliability from a single adminis-tration of a single form of a test is applicable to tests in which speed of performance has an appreciable effect upon test score. In the extreme case, for example, if the split-half method is applied to a speeded test so easy that essentially no errors are made, the estimated reliability coefficient automatically will be very close to 1.00, no matter what the intrinsic char-acteristics of the test that might affect temporal instability.

The inclusion of this discussion of reliability and of techniques for esti-mating it is not intended to imply that the teacher will automatically and systematically estimate the reliability of every test that he gives. On the other hand, he may well wish to investigate the reliability of occasional tests. In any event, one who is answerable for assigning academic marks has a responsibility for understanding possible sources of unreliability in his marks.

THE CONCEPT OF TEST VALIDITY

The reliability of a test or the accuracy with which it measures some-thing in a particular group is one aspect of the *validity* of the test. The concept of validity refers to the extent to which the test serves its purpose with respect to the group for which it is intended.

Relation of Validity to Reliability

If the test is not measuring whatever it measures consistently, then it cannot be valid for any purpose. On the other hand, it may measure some-thing with a high degree of reliability without being at all useful for the purpose for which it is intended. In other words, a test may have even a perfect degree of reliability and no validity whatever for some particular use. A test of a given degree of reliability will ordinarily have different validities for different purposes. Thus the concept of validity makes sense only if we specify the purpose. Note, moreover, that the notion of purpose here must include the group which is to take the test.

Ways of Appraising Validity

Writers on the topic of validity have begun to talk about different kinds of validity. Some have differentiated *empirical* or *statistical* validity and *logical* or *curricular* validity. Committees of the American Psychological

Association, the American Educational Research Association, and the National Council on Measurements Used in Education have distinguished four kinds of validity: predictive, concurrent, construct, and content. From one point of view, these are not different kinds of validity. Rather, the distinctions arise from different methods of assessing validity. The basic question is always the extent to which the test serves its purpose.

The concern of the teacher in using a test of educational achievement is ultimately with the relation of responses on the test questions to responses in some universe of situations that will be encountered by the student later. In some instances, a measure of behavior in this universe of later situations can be obtained and the behavior score in the test situation correlated with the measure of performance that the test was intended to predict. If this relationship is expressed in terms of a correlation coefficient, we may then speak of it as a *validity coefficient*. This is what is meant by reference to empirical validity, statistical validity, or predictive validity. The measure of the behavior or a sampling of behavior from a universe of situations with which one is concerned is called a *criterion measure*.

Differences among Criteria

Not all criterion measures are equally satisfactory. They, too, may differ in reliability. In the extreme case, if the criterion measure has no reliability there is no point in attempting to predict it. Paradoxically, criterion measures also differ in *validity* or relevance to the ultimate goal of the test. Thus the ultimate aim of a battery of tests of nursing aptitude might be regarded as success in a nursing career. One might then think of some index of success in the field, say, ten years after graduation from the nursing curriculum. But such an index would be difficult, if not impossible, to get. One then might hit upon the notion that graduation from a nursing curriculum is one step toward a career in nursing and adopt some index of performance in a school of nursing as a criterion against which to assess the value of the aptitude tests. This criterion clearly differs from the index of success in a career in nursing. Such a measure, which falls short of the ultimate one, is sometimes referred to as a *proximate criterion*.

Substitutes for Empirical Study of Validity

For the vast majority of teacher-made educational achievement tests, no investigation of predictive validity will be feasible. In the lack of an independent criterion measure, other attacks on the validity question are made. Without a criterion, a validity coefficient for a test cannot be computed. Hence the statistical or empirical predictive validity cannot be explored directly. This does not mean that the tester becomes interested primarily in a different kind of validity but rather that he uses different methods in providing reasonable assurance that the test will serve its purpose. At this point, writers begin to speak of logical validity, curricular validity, validity by definition, and, especially in recent years, *content validity*.

By content validity, they do not wish to imply that the test constructor or user is no longer concerned with the later, out-of-school behavior of the subjects in some universe of situations. They mean, rather, that inferences as to the degree of correspondence between behavior in the test situation and later behavior are to be made without resort to direct comparisons. The test constructor, for example, might outline in considerable detail course content and objectives in terms of mental operations or processes. Then he would attempt to demonstrate the extent to which the content and types of responses required in the test situation sample or parallel those encompassed in the course objectives. This approach requires an explicit statement of the objectives of the educational unit involved. The sampling of the situations presented in the test exercises must be representative of the universe to which inferences are to be generalized.

Fortunately a test may have acceptable content validity without comprising the entire set of situations included in course objectives. Often, resort to a sampling of these is equally satisfactory and considerably more efficient.

The Necessity for Judgment

A test may appear to have excellent validity with respect to the immediate objectives of a unit of instruction when these are ill-conceived in relation to more nearly ultimate educational goals. In fact, one of the major advantages of attention to the development of educational tests is the highlighting of what may be weaknesses in course objectives.

Whether one thinks in terms of predicting an external criterion or in terms of sampling curriculum content and objectives in an effective way, *the necessity for human judgment at some point is inescapable*. In the case of predictive validity, the decision must be made that the criterion is itself valid. Other judgments are entailed in deciding how to get usable measures of the criterion itself. In respect to content validity, judgment is applied more directly to the question of the relationship between the behavior in the test situation and in the universe of behavior comprising the goals. The test constructor cannot avoid this responsibility. Not all judgment is equally good, however. That based on thorough consideration of the purposes of the test, with analysis into detailed components, is the most useful.

Validity, then, entails the questions both of whether the test is adequately serving its ultimate purpose and of how accurately it is measuring. If recourse can be had to an independent measure of the criterion itself and if the correlation between the test measures and the criterion measures is satisfactorily high, the question of the reliability of the test measures may not need to be explored separately. When the empirical validity is low, however, a check on reliability may reveal that the trouble lies in the inconsistency of the test measures themselves. Sometimes steps can be taken, as, for example, lengthening the test through the addition of more comparable items, to improve the reliability and thus the empirical validity.

In case no independent criterion is obtainable, so that one must resort to immediate judgment as to the validity of the test measures, the professional test constructor often estimates the reliability of the test scores simply to avoid unreliability as a source of low validity. Although the ordinary teacher does not obtain an estimate of the reliability of every test he uses, he should investigate the reliability coefficients of enough tests to provide an adequate experiential basis for a reasonable degree of confidence in the reliability of other tests for which this characteristic is not to be systematically explored.

Also, as will be clear by now, the typical teacher is not usually in a position to obtain empirical measures of the validity of his tests. But there is no excuse for his ignoring the practicality of a systematic analysis of the objectives of the unit of instruction in question and taking minimal precautions to ensure a representative sampling of appropriate content and behavioral processes.[3]

---

[3]Further suggestions for achieving this kind of assurance of test validity are provided in chapter 6.

Chapter 4

The Role of Objective Measures in Academic Achievement Testing

Much has been written in the last thirty or forty years to encourage the use of objective tests of academic achievement. Some of this writing has penetrated the curriculum of schools of education and special courses in departments of psychology. Relatively little, however, has had any lasting effect upon teachers, especially at the college level. At some point early in their teaching careers they may encounter good advice and even assistance in developing testing practices; or they may be able to recall and try to adapt some approaches to testing to which they were exposed as students. Too often, they come to look upon test questions themselves as chores to be dispensed with as quickly as possible and on the laborious grading of responses to questions as a necessary evil. In reviewing types of tests that might be appropriate, they may associate unpleasant emotional connotations with some unfortunately contrived true-false test items and at once dismiss all thought of attempting to construct good objective tests.

A weak objective test may indeed provide less valid results than a poorly constructed essay test—and let it not be overlooked that many of the latter are indeed sorry. Nevertheless, a good objective test, which is by no means to be dashed off in a short evening's work, may provide considerably greater assurance of validity than accompanies a well-constructed essay test.

Chances are that most persons engaged in teaching will find occasion to use both sorts of tests. For this reason, attention is given in this book to principles and practices that may, it is hoped, lead to improvements in examining devices in general. Since the readers will probably have more to gain from greater attention to objective tests because they have had less experience with them both as subjects and as examiners than with essay tests, more specific attention will be given to the development of objective tests. In chapter 10, however, suggestions will be made for improving essay tests, particularly with respect to their scoring.

Several important characteristics of an objective test should be noted:

1. *Reliability*. Objective tests can much more readily be made reliable in their scoring than can essay tests. One of the important sources of potential unreliability of psychological measuring devices can be controlled almost completely in objective tests. This is that portion of unreliability due to scorer inconsistencies. It includes both the inconsistency of one scorer from one occasion to another and the disagreement that may occur among different scorers if the scoring must depend upon variable judgments. This objectivity of the scoring has led to the term *objective test*.

While different experts may disagree on the right answer to an objective question in the first analysis, the source of the disagreement can be pinpointed and the question often repaired. Should disagreement persist, the question is not an objective one and must be discarded. By and large, however, it is possible to construct questions which would be answered alike by authorities presumed to be equally competent. The key for an objective test can be determined in advance so that any person with a reasonable degree of clerical ability can perform the actual scoring. Even when a test cannot be tried out on a group of typical subjects before it must be used in an actual testing situation, techniques exist for detecting unf reseen blunders in the scoring key. (See chapter 9.)

2. *Scoring Economy*. The scoring of an objective test can be done by an inexpensive clerk. More important, however, when clerical help is not at hand the teacher can complete the scoring of an objective test in a fraction of the time that would be required for an essay test that involved equal testing time. Thus one can accomplish in an hour or so a task that otherwise would have required days. No small advantage of this difference

is the fact that test results can be made available to the students in very short order, and this has important motivational implications, as noted in chapter 2.

The construction of an objective test may take considerably more time than a teacher commonly devotes to the preparation of an essay test. To develop the first few objective tests in a field is indeed time-consuming. As the teacher begins to use such tests and develops a file of items that can be employed again in different combinations, however, the construction of an objective test is by no means so inordinately time-consuming as it may at first appear.

The relative saving in scoring time with objective tests is proportionately greater the larger the number of students to be tested. This point is sometimes overstressed, however. Once the teacher becomes accustomed to a file of usable items so that he does not have to start *de novo* on each new test, the scoring advantages of objective tests seem appreciable even for very small classes.

Teachers who have adopted objective tests without guidance have often been unaware of some of the techniques that will facilitate scoring. This matter will be treated further in chapter 6.

3. *Adequacy of Content Sampling.* What seems to many to be the principal virtue of objective tests, in contrast to essay tests, is that they can much more adequately sample the universe of subject-matter content and of types of behavior constituting the goals of a particular unit of the curriculum. Think, for example, of a fifty-minute essay test that may consist of three or four broad questions, often not very explicitly framed. Compare this with an objective test that may contain as many as sixty or seventy questions, each presented with five possible answers. In most cases, the objective test will clearly provide a distinctly more complete and representative coverage of the universe of situations that might have been sampled in the testing period.

With the objective test, the student cannot find himself in the position of luckily being asked the three questions that he knew and not being asked the three or four major questions that he failed to study. Nor, of course, will he find himself in the position of being confronted with just the few questions on which he was weak. With an objective test, the student should have no grounds for feeling either lucky or unlucky with respect to the choice of questions if the test is at all carefully assembled. He may, of course, object for other reasons. Specifically, he may demur because he has to pinpoint his responses in an objective fashion and is thus unable to clothe his ignorance with verbiage. Moreover, he can sometimes make the legitimate complaint that a poorly constructed objective test is over-emphasizing memorization of specific factual content. But ordinarily he cannot find fault with the sampling of the test.

Note the importance of a representative sampling of content. Mere random sampling is by no means sufficient. Three essay questions may be chosen at random from a hundred or so possible essay questions, but they can scarcely be regarded as adequately sampling the universe of content that makes up the course. Moreover, one may strongly suspect that the sampling is more likely to be biased in the case of essay tests, which are too often constructed by the teacher on his way to class and thus likely to be influenced by such factors as the law of recency.

Chapter 5

Common Types of Objective Test Items

Several types of objective test items will be more or less familiar to the reader, who will need to be aware of the differentiating characteristics of each major type. Although rules for constructing objective test items will later be presented in terms of multiple-choice items, many of the principles can be applied to other kinds of items.

TRUE-FALSE ITEMS

Probably the most familiar type of objective test item, the true-false, has least to recommend it.

One of its drawbacks is that the item constructor is too likely simply to adopt verbatim statements from a textbook, with perhaps the inclusion of some negative terms to make some of the items false. Such a practice encourages rote memorization on the part of the student. Moreover, it tends to limit the testing to factual details.

A second major disadvantage lies in the difficulty of incorporating in the item itself the standard of truth or falsity against which the item is to be judged by the subject. The relative degree of truth of a statement may be regarded as lying somewhere along a continuum. The person judging how to respond to the item has to decide not only how far it lies to the right or to the left of the continuum of truth as he visualizes it but also how far it must lie in one direction or the other to agree with the item writer's conception of truth or falsity. When, on the other hand, he is presented essentially with several statements, as in a multiple-choice item, his task may be regarded as one of ordering the alternative statements along a continuum and selecting as his answer the one that is nearest to one extreme of the continuum. This point is worth elaboration. Suppose that an item constructor presents as a true-false item the following statement:

> The most essential characteristic of a psychological test is accuracy of measurement.

The hypothetical item constructor intended this item to be false. Although some degree of reliability is essential in a test, the most important characteristic is validity or the extent to which the test serves its intended purpose. Reading his item outside of any context, however, one might argue that certainly the statement as presented does not refer to the worst conceivable characteristic of a test, and, furthermore, that it even deals with a necessary condition. He might therefore mark the item true.

Efforts of the item writer who attempts to avoid this weakness and who yet insists upon limiting his efforts to the true-false form often culminate in items that are undeniably true or false. These of necessity are largely factual in nature. Perhaps such efforts to overcome a basic fault of true-false items account in large part for the criticism that objective tests place too much emphasis upon memory for facts.

A third undesirable feature of true-false items, which may be related to the second objection raised, is that they often lead to emotional reactions. Students may also recoil from such items because they are thought to be testing merely factual knowledge. In any event, students often complete a true-false examination with the feeling that it has been grossly unfair in its appraisal of what they really know or can do.

MULTIPLE-CHOICE ITEMS

One of the basic characteristics of a multiple-choice item is that the item itself contains the standard by means of which the best answer is to be selected. Supposing that the illustrative true-false item used above were recast into a multiple-choice form, it might appear as follows:

The most essential characteristic of a psychological test is

(1) the adequacy with which it serves its purpose;

(2) accuracy of measurement;

(3) its acceptability to the subjects as a valid test;

(4) accuracy of scoring;

(5) its complete coverage of the area concerned.

The standard of truth that precludes the second answer (which, with the problem, is equivalent to the true-false item above) becomes immediately obvious.

One further advantage of the multiple-choice form arises from the fact that the best answer does not have to be the one and only indisputably correct response to the question posed. It must, however, be defensible as the best among the alternatives presented. This characteristic allows the item constructor much more latitude in the selection of concepts to be tested by multiple-choice items than he is permitted for true-false items. Thus he can present several items on some one important problem. Also, he can sometimes produce a more discriminating item than is the case if he confines himself to the one most nearly perfect answer to a question.

The problem can be posed either as a direct question or as an incomplete statement. The answer can be agreed upon ahead of time by authorities in the field, so that the scoring can be completely objective. Problems of a great degree of complexity can be couched in the multiple-choice form, which is by no means limited to the presentation of factual items only.

The multiple-choice form is very flexible. Several sets of multiple-choice questions can be based on the same situation, or several different items can be answered by choice from among the same set of alternatives. Numerous variants of the multiple-choice form are exemplified in Appendix C. On the whole, the multiple-choice form has all of the advantages of scoring objectivity and none of the drawbacks of true-false items.

MATCHING ITEMS

So-called matching items are really a variant of the multiple-choice form in which, for each of several items, choice is made from among the same set of alternatives. The items might consist, for example, of several terms to be defined, while the alternative answers would consist of definitions. Although the typical instructions might be to the effect that the subject is to match one item from a list at the right to one item at the left, basically his task is to scan the alternatives at the right and select one to go with each item at the left.

Two common faults in the construction of matching items warrant mention. One is to have the same number of elements in each list (that is, the same number of items as there are alternatives). Since with such a set of items the typical procedure is to have each answer apply once only, the subject who knows the answers to all but one of the items will automatically get this one correct also. Similarly, the subject who knows all but two has an increased probability of getting the two correct as compared with other multiple-choice items that may be included in the test; etc. This difficulty can be readily avoided by one of two methods. The first is to include in the list of alternatives a greater number of elements than there are items. A second solution that can sometimes be applied is to provide that the same alternative may be the answer to more than one of the items. If this method is to work, some of the alternatives must in fact be used in this way.

A second mistake that commonly appears in the use of matching items is to include far too many elements in both lists. This means that the subject must scrutinize a long list, which almost certainly contains some completely implausible answers, as he approaches each item in the other list. In a long list there is very likely to be a lack of homogeneity in the alternatives. For example, when the answers include dates, names, and definitions, clearly the dates could not possibly be the correct responses to certain of the items. The subject is unnecessarily annoyed when he is forced to go down the list to find answers in the correct field before he narrows his choice. This difficulty can be readily overcome by presenting sets of homogeneous items in separate lists.

RANK-ORDER ITEMS

A type of item that may present special scoring problems may be called the rank-order item. Here the problem of the subject is to indicate for the elements presented their appropriate order, perhaps chronological or logical. Suppose, for example, that the correct order for five elements presented as A, B, C, D, and E is 5, 3, 1, 2, 4. Such a problem has actually been included in commercial tests as five items, with the scoring key to the first item presented as 5, to the second as 3, to the next as 1, to the next as 2, and to the last as 4. Now consider what happens to the student who responds 4, 5, 3, 1, 2. He misses all five items. Yet in a way he has as much information as the student who answers 5, 1, 3, 2, 4, who would get three points, or as much as the student who gets three points by responding 5, 3, 1, 4, 2. One can readily find other odd examples of seeming inequities.

Far more reasonable scoring plans can be devised. For example, one could set down each possible pattern of responses or orders indicated by the responses the students might make and compute the correlation coefficient between each possible ordering and the correct order.[1] Then the response to the set of items would appropriately be regarded as a unit and a total number of points assigned that would be proportional to the correlation with the correct order. Such a plan is not difficult to understand but rather awkward to apply, especially for any sizeable number of subjects. Hence some other alternative should be sought, especially since the suggested plan obviates any mechanical aids to scoring such as scoring machines.

Another possibility is to present for each scoring unit a smaller number of elements to be placed in order, say three. There are of course six possible answers. One might then argue that the set can be scored as a unit—that is, one point might be given if the order for three elements is correct, and no points if it is incorrect. Such an argument is sometimes applied when problems of this type are to be combined with five-choice multiple-choice items, it being noted that the chance of getting an item of the latter type correct is one in five whereas the chance of getting the order of three

---

[1]The simplest type of coefficient would be the rank-difference correlation coefficient, which is discussed in most elementary statistics books.

things correct is one in six. If one wished to use a scoring stencil or machine-scoring based on a maximum of five choices, he could himself rule out one of the six orders that appears to him least plausible and then present as five choices the five other possible orderings of the three elements.

Whatever solution one adopts to the scoring problem, he should be aware of the pitfalls if he chooses to use rank-order items.

COMPLETION ITEMS

Completion items by rights should not be included in the treatment of objective test items. Yet, because the answers to them are typically short, and because the scoring may be more objective than in the case of ordinary essay items, they are most commonly regarded as one of the types of objective items.

Completion items may take two forms. They may be simply short-answer questions, with an answer of a single word or a short phrase to be given; or they may consist of sentences with one or more internal blanks to be filled in by the subject with a word or a short phrase. In either case, they lack two of the important advantages of objective tests: the scoring is not nearly so routine and it is not maximally objective. Unless the teacher is to insist that there is a single way of expressing the answer—a practice in general to be deplored—he cannot ordinarily anticipate the variant correct answers that will be given. Hence the scoring cannot be turned over to anyone else, and it will take considerably more of his time than would a more objective form of test.

Completion items rather readily assume absurd forms. The writer recalls having seen one item that went exactly as follows:

_____, working with_____, discovered_____.

Presumably, students who had made an exact transcript of what the lecturer said were able to call up the correct associations with the minimal clues provided in the item.

Those who favor completion items may argue that they test the more important process of recall rather than recognition. All that seems necessary to counter this argument is to point out that a number of early studies in the field of testing demonstrated conclusively that equally well-constructed tests of recall and of recognition were so highly correlated that they clearly were testing the same basic factors.

Chapter 6

Planning an Objective Test

DEFINING THE OBJECTIVES OF THE TEST

Too often a test is hastily assembled from materials that happen to be readily available or from ideas that chance to be uppermost in the mind of the teacher. Any semblance of a test plan under such circumstances emerges by induction from the materials that were placed in the test. The procedure should rather be reversed, the specifications for the test first being carefully formulated and then the test materials selected or produced to conform to the plan.

The development of a test outline calls for a rather detailed consideration of the objectives of the unit of instruction, course, or broader segment of the educational process. One procedure that is often recommended is to set up a two-way table with one axis to represent subject-matter content and the other the types of behavior or mental processes that the test is intended to elicit. Then each of these two broad categories is subdivided into anywhere from four or five to as many as ten or twelve categories, depending partly on the nature of the unit of instruction together with the complexity of its objectives and partly upon the degree of detail in which the examiner wishes to perceive his test. One may choose along each axis three or four broad categories and then indicate several subdivisions of each of these. A particular cell in the table may then be used to record the number (or percentage) of items that fall within the horizontal and vertical categories that intersect at the cell in question. Two such outlines are illustrated in the following charts.

CHART OF A COMPREHENSIVE EXAMINATION IN BIOLOGICAL SCIENCE

OBJECTIVES ↘ CONTENT	I To achieve a knowledge and understanding of			II Scientific thinking as evidenced by ability to			
	A. a working vocabulary. (7% of the items)	B. biological concepts and principles. (35% of the items)	C. related reading. (8% of the items)	A. recognize and solve problems. (15% of the items)	B. recognize hypotheses and select methods of testing them. (5% of the items)	C. critically evaluate experimental procedures, data, conclusions, and implications. (15% of the items)	D. appraise real situations. (15% of the items)
Characteristics common to all living things	4% of the total items →			3% of the total items →			
Maintenance of the individual 1. Food production and utilization 2. Transport and excretion 3. Coordination and adjustment	17% of the total items →			18% of the total items →			
Maintenance of the species 1. Reproduction 2. Heredity	12% of the total items →			12% of the total items →			
History of life on the earth	5% of the total items →			4% of the total items →			
Interrelationships 1. Ecological relations 2. Parasitism and disease 3. Classification	12% of the total items →			13% of the total items →			
	This represents 50% of the examination.			This represents 50% of the examination.			

Reprinted by permission from Paul L. Dressel et al., Comprehensive Examinations in a Program of General Education (East Lansing: Michigan State University Press, 1949), p. 48.

CHART OF AN EXAMINATION IN HISTORY OF CIVILIZATION

CONTENT / OBJECTIVES	I Nature of Civilization	II Hellenic Civilization	III Hellenistic Civilization	IV Roman Civilization	V Medieval Civilization, the Church	VI Medieval Civilization, Feudalism	VII The Medieval Mind	VIII The Renaissance	IX The Reformation	X The 18th Century	XI The French Revolution	XII The Last Century	TOTAL
Knowledge and Understanding of													
1. Historical Terms	—	2	1	1	3	—	1	2	1	5	5	4	25
2. Cause-Effect Relationships	1	1	—	3	2	3	4	1	6	3	3	3	30
3. Motivating Ideals	—	1	—	1	6	5	6	1	10	3	1	7	41
4. Miscellaneous	9	11	4	6	4	6	12	9	5	8	11	13	98
Ability to													
5. Recognize Chronological Relationships	—	5	1	3	5	—	3	1	1	1	2	3	25
6. Use Historical Maps	—	—	2	1	2	1	—	2	1	6	3	5	23
7. Evaluate Differences in Civilizations	1	4	1	1	1	1	6	—	—	5	6	6	32
8. Read Historical Materials	—	—	—	5	—	6	—	5	—	—	—	10	26
TOTAL	11	24	9	21	23	22	32	21	24	31	31	51	300

Use of a two-way outline helps to ensure adequate coverage of the field in question, with respect to both specific content and the type of student behavior that is to be manifested. For example, the examiner is helped to avoid overemphasizing areas of subject matter that he happens to like better than others, and he can readily see the extent to which his test will depend heavily upon factual memorization.

As the test-maker gains experience and no longer needs to fear that his tests will fail to tap some of the higher thought processes, he may be satisfied to depend upon a one-way outline of subject-matter content. This will probably be true, for example, if he is thoroughly familiar with the types of items from which he can make selections in the various content subdivisions. Even though he may no longer rely very often upon a two-way outline, the teacher should take stock of the mental processes thought to be involved in a selection of items before endorsing it.

A one-way outline is illustrated on page 35. Note that it will frequently be desirable to include some categories for items that do not fit into other selected categories. These may be labeled "Miscellaneous" or "Other." Their use will permit a degree of flexibility in assembling test items and make possible the use of some good items that otherwise might not fall into any of the listed categories. However, if the test outline is to be used to construct more than one form of the test, in such a way that different forms may be used as equivalent or interchangeably, the categories should be sufficiently narrow so that every item that one wishes to include can be catalogued. This will help to ensure that different forms of the test are selected to the same specifications.

WEIGHTING TEST COMPONENTS

The test outline, as noted above, indicates the number of items falling into each category. This applies to both the horizontal and the vertical categories in case a two-way outline is used. These numbers will provide rough indications of the importance or weight of each category in the total test. The question of the relative weight of elements in a composite, as, for example, when test items are combined to yield a score on the total test, is somewhat complicated. While this is not the place to elaborate the technicalities, the reader should at least be aware that the real or effective

A ONE-WAY OUTLINE FOR A TEST
ON ACHIEVEMENT TEST DEVELOPMENT

Area of Content		Number of Items
(a) Measurement principles		4
1—Origin	2	
2—Units	2	
(b) Reliability		8
1—Definition and Concepts	3	
2—Methods of Appraising	5	
(c) Validity		11
1—Definition and Concepts	3	
2—Methods of Appraising	4	
3—Relation to Reliability	2	
4—Criteria for	2	
(d) Forms of Objective Tests		11
1—True-False	2	
2—Completion	2	
3—Matching	2	
4—Rank-Order	2	
5—Multiple-Choice	3	
(e) Principles for Constructing Multiple-Choice Tests		20
1—The Item as a Whole	5	
2—The Problem	5	
3—The Alternatives	10	
(f) Elementary Statistical Methods		15
1—Frequency Distributions	2	
2—Measures of Central Tendency	4	
3—Measures of Variability	4	
4—Measures of Correlation	5	
(g) Item Analysis		8
1—Difficulty	2	
2—Discriminating Power	6	
(h) The Essay Test		10
1—Advantages	3	
2—Disadvantages	3	
3—Ways of Improving	4	
(i) Miscellaneous	13	13
Totals	100	100

weights of different components are not always what they appear to be.

For one thing, the contribution of a component to the total score depends partly upon how variable the scores on the component itself are. In an extreme case, if all students get the same score on an item or a group of items considered as a part of a total test, the effect of this component is simply to add a constant amount to the score of every individual. Or, in case all students miss an item or get zero points on a group of items, from the standpoint of learning anything about the individual differences in the group of subjects, this component has contributed nothing whatever. To be sure, motivational purposes sometimes dictate the inclusion in a test of some items so easy that all students will get a perfect score on them. While such items may be effective as an instructional device, they are deadwood as far as measurement is concerned.

A second characteristic of a test component that is related to its effective weight is the degree of its relationship to other components. For example, among the abilities for which a test is designed may be "drawing conclusions from evidence" and "recognition of the tentative nature of conclusions." If these abilities are in fact correlated among the students or if the test constructor has been able to make little distinction between them, then their positive correlation will mean that each ability, considered singly, is receiving more weight than is apparent in the mere number of items shown in the test outline. True, other things being equal, the relative weight of the set of items varies with the number of items. But other things may not be equal, and often the time and statistical facilities for exploring the relative variabilities of parts of a test and their interrelationships with other parts are unavailable.

USE OF STATISTICAL DATA IN TEST PLANNING

Once a teacher begins to take seriously his responsibility for appraising the progress of students, he may begin to develop some minimal statistical information about the individual items that he has used. This information would typically include some simple index of the difficulty of the item, such as the percentage of the subjects who got the correct answer, and perhaps some measure of the relationship of the item to the total test of which it is a part. (See chapter 9.) If the teacher is assembling a test from a file of items on which such information is available, he may then refine his test planning by taking account of the difficulty and discriminating power of the individual items. Suppose that a test is to be given to a new group of students comparable in abilities and in the type of educational situations to which they have been exposed. Then from the average percentage of students who previously passed each item, one can predict with a fair degree of accuracy the average score on the newly assembled test. Thus if the average difficulty percentage of the sixty items used in a test is 58 per cent, the average score of the new but comparable students on the test will be approximately 58 per cent of sixty, or about thirty-five items.

PLANNING OPTIMAL TEST DIFFICULTY

The matter of planning examinations should not be left without explicit mention of the fact that most educational achievement tests are too easy to be optimally effective as measuring devices. This may be partly attributable to the fallacious belief of many teachers that passing marks should be between 70 per cent and 100 per cent of whatever items happen to be given in tests. The practice of making tests too easy at the cost of efficiency of measurement may also, upon occasion, be attributed to a desire to provide positive motivation. With proper interpretation to students of the arbitrary nature of raw scores on tests, however, the tests can be made more difficult without sacrificing this instructional goal.

From the standpoint of effective testing, the teacher should ordinarily aim to have the average score on the test approximately equal to 50 per cent of the items. This means that the average difficulty of the items should be such that 50 per cent of the students get them right and 50 per cent get them wrong. Ordinarily it is recommended that, while the average difficulty be 50 per cent, the items vary in difficulty through a range of perhaps 15 per cent to 85 per cent. Note, however, that the most efficient single item, from the standpoint of the amount of information that it provides about individual differences, is one passed by 50 per cent and failed by 50 per cent. (See also pp. 81-82.)

When tests are pitched at a level of difficulty such that the average score on the test will be 80 or 85, information about the relative differences among the subjects that could be obtained from a more difficult test is lost In exceptional circumstances an extremely difficult test may be indicated, as would be the case if one were selecting a very small percentage of scholarship applicants. A very easy test may be most efficient, on the other hand, when the extremely slow learners are to be chosen for intensive remedial instruction.

SPECIAL INSTRUCTIONS FOR A TEST

Test planning must also take into account any need for special instructions to the subjects and to the examiners unless the test constructor himself is to give the test. Often in the case of a classroom test, the students become so accustomed to a particular type of test that they will require no special instructions on the kind of item included and the manner in which they are to indicate their answers. If the teacher is using a type of test likely to be unfamiliar to some students, however, he must be meticulous in making sure that the students understand the type of question and exactly how the questions are to be answered. Sometimes it is helpful to include a sample of each type of item used. Many standardized tests present one or two examples with the answers already marked and then several which the subjects themselves are to answer. When some students fail to understand the types of questions used, a significant portion of the variance in the test scores may be attributable to differences in the readiness with which the students perceive the instructions.

PLANNING EFFICIENT TEST SCORING

The test planner should be aware of some of the simple devices that will facilitate the scoring of an objective test. Significant saving in scoring time results when answers are recorded on a separate answer sheet so that some sort of scoring stencil can be applied. For items such that the answers can be indicated by marking one of not more than five positions for each item, a very useful plan is to have the answers marked on IBM special answer sheets. Then a scoring key can be made in such a way that holes indicate the position of the correct answer. When such a stencil is applied to an answer sheet, the pencil marks that show through the holes can readily be counted (whether or not they are marked with colored pencil for later use in discussing the test with students). If more than perhaps 200 (and possibly as few as 100 or 150) answer sheets are to be scored, the teacher can often obtain convenient access to an IBM scoring machine, which will yield the scores quickly. Since the machines are not 100 per cent accurate, especially on humid days, some teachers may still prefer to use hand-scoring even for fairly large numbers of students. As the teacher who uses such a machine will soon learn, it is quite adaptable and can be made to weight items appearing in certain sections of the answer sheet by a predetermined arbitrary multiplier. It can even be set to apply one of the formulas that is sometimes used for "correction for guessing" (see below) by automatically subtracting a fraction of the number of wrong answers from the number of right answers.

If a test is not adaptable to one of the manufactured answer sheets, one specially designed and duplicated for particular tests often more than repays its cost. Any type of device that saves turning the pages of the question booklet itself and keeping in mind or separately recording part scores for each page will prove to be a great convenience that sometimes does not occur to a teacher. In some instances a separate answer sheet is considered undesirable, as when speed of test performance is at a premium. Then the spaces for answers may be placed in a column to the right or left of each page of the question booklet, so that a strip stencil can be placed alongside the answer spaces to provide ready comparisons.

THE QUESTION OF "CORRECTION FOR GUESSING"

Mention was made above of "correction for guessing." Almost any person who begins to use objective tests soon encounters some opinion to the effect that he ought to be correcting the scores for chance success. This is one of the most misused concepts in the field of testing, especially as it has been applied to classroom tests. Most such tests are, or should be, of such a nature that the student has a reasonable opportunity to read all the items and indicate his answers in the time allotted. Such tests are sometimes called *power tests*, as distinguished from *speed tests*.

True, situations arise, especially in skills testing at the elementary school level, in which it is important to test the speed of presumably routinized responses. Thus a test consisting of items of the elementary addition combinations would commonly be given with a severe time limit, so that even the most rapid adders would not be expected to complete the test. If it were given in a time period so long that every subject had an opportunity to read every item in a fairly leisurely fashion and respond to it, the expectation would be that the scores would pile up at the high end of the scale. The information about individual differences provided by the test would be minimal. With such a test, the mere number of right answers tends to give an undue advantage to the rapid, careless student who may even respond to the items without reading them. Then, simply by chance, he may expect to get a certain proportion of the items correct, depending upon how many alternatives are presented for each item. Thus, with a true-false or two-choice test, he could expect to get on the average about 50 per cent of the items correct if he paid no attention whatever to the content of the items. By marking fifty such items in a random fashion, he may get about as good a score as the meticulous student who carefully answers the first twenty-five of the items correctly and never gets to the last half of the test. The scoring situation can be improved by applying in this case the formula

$$\text{score} = \text{number right} - \text{number wrong,}$$

which may be abbreviated

$$S = R - W.$$

Now the student who simply guessed at all fifty items will get a score, on the average, of twenty-five minus twenty-five, or zero. Although some such students will get scores greater and some less than zero, on the average the formula will assign a zero score to the person who guesses at all answers.

The foregoing formula is a special case of a more general formula for multiple-choice scoring, in which the score is computed by subtracting from the number of right answers the number of wrong answers divided by the number of choices per item less one. This formula can be expressed as

$$S = R - \frac{W}{n-1}$$

Here R is the number of right answers, W is the number of wrong answers (excluding omitted items); n equals the number of choices per item; and S, the score, is an estimate of the number of answers known among the items attempted and hence is the score corrected for chance success.[1]

Especially note that this formula is of no practical value whatever in the typical classroom testing situation in which practically all the students

---

[1]Dorothy C. Adkins *et al.*, *Construction and Analysis of Achievement Tests* (Washington, D. C.: U. S. Civil Service Commission, 1947), pp. 188–89.

have an opportunity to read and respond to every item. When all students answer all items a perfect relationship exists between the number of correct answers and scores obtained by using the correction-for-errors scoring formula or, in fact, by adding to or subtracting from the number of right answers any multiple whatever of the number of wrong answers. While the teacher may believe there is some pedagogical advantage to providing the students with some estimate of the number of answers they *knew* instead of merely the number of answers that were correct, nothing is to be gained by correcting for errors in this fashion from the standpoint of measurement in the case of power tests.

As indicated above, the situation is quite different when the test places a premium on speed. Only when the fastest and presumably best students cannot possibly complete the test is there any useful information about individual differences among the students provided by the use of scoring formulas of this type. This situation is rare once one gets beyond the elementary school level. Use of correction-for-errors formulas should be reserved for tests in which there is some possibility that the validity of the tests might thereby be raised.

USE OF OPTIONAL ITEMS

Still another question to be considered in planning tests is related to the use of optional items, a practice much more common for essay than for objective tests. This difference is understandable, largely because the use of optional items is sometimes thought to help to compensate for the inadequate sampling of essay tests. For objective tests, with much larger and presumably representative sampling of the desired content and processes, little need exists for special devices to compensate for poor sampling.

The use of optional items, as when students are instructed to answer any three of four questions, has one decided drawback. This is simply that they are not really taking the same test, so that any attempt to appraise them by means of the same measuring scale is at once defeated.

It is sometimes claimed, as for example in Ph. D. written comprehensive examinations, that the answers are somehow to be appraised irrespective of their specific content. Hence the particular questions do not make much difference, it is argued, except to the poor student who may become emotionally distraught if faced with a question that arouses feelings of inadequacy. The supposed solution is that this irrelevant source of variability should be removed by presenting wider latitude in the specific content of the answers to the questions, since in any case attention is to be focused upon fundamentally more important abilities such as thinking, handling abstract ideas, organizing materials, marshaling relevant evidence, etc. Yet that the different questions from which the students are permitted to choose are likely to bring these different abilities into play to exactly the same extent is extremely doubtful. The conclusion is that the responses cannot readily be evaluated on the same measuring scale. A more legitimate point of view in the case of graduate degree examinations is that the students have been exposed to different curricula, so that identical examinations are inappropriate. The same universe of content should not be sampled for all candidates. Hence, although several may be examined at the same time for purposes of convenience, the pretense that they are taking the same examination when choice of questions is permitted should be abandoned.

No legitimate reason can be advanced for applying the notion of optional items to the ordinary test, whether it be essay or objective.

Chapter 7

Constructing Objective Test Items

Although some books on objective tests present separate principles for the construction of each type of item, this practice involves much repetition. Here the general rules will be presented in terms of multiple-choice items. Their extensions to other types of objective items or to one of the many special cases of multiple-choice items will be apparent to the reader. The illustrations for the most part will be variants of the same problem or question regardless of the principle being exemplified. By this device, the risk of distracting attention from the rule being discussed will be reduced and the reader will not be subjected to the annoyance of attempting to understand a particular principle of item writing from an illustration couched in subject matter that may be foreign to him. Insofar as possible, the underlying content of the multiple-choice item on page 26 will be used to exemplify the points being discussed here.

REQUISITES FOR ITEM WRITING

Rare indeed is the teacher so fortunate as to have an assistant with both the time and the talent for item construction. Ordinarily, it is a task to which his own efforts must be turned. Several requisites of the successful item writer include a thorough knowledge of the subject matter; an intimate understanding of specific teaching objectives; an insight into the backgrounds, abilities, and particularly the mental processes of the subjects who are to take the test; a facility in the clear and economical use of language; and, perhaps above all, an essential willingness to devote the time and energy necessary to the task. The item writer does not need to be adept at creative writing of the imaginative sort required, say, for the production of a short story or a sonnet. He does require skill in expository writing. He need not sit idly while awaiting inspirations for items. Rather, he may actively stimulate ideas by constant reference to written materials such as textbooks, periodicals, course outlines, lecture notes, and the like.

Some beginning item writers seem to work quite productively for the first day or so, writing many more items than would normally constitute a good quota. Then they may be caught up short, after their more ready inspirations have been committed to paper, and reach a nonproductive plateau that can be overcome only by turning to external sources for item ideas. Some persons, once they have overcome their initial blocking, can produce items steadily day after day and even make a living by this means. Others, however, are never satisfied to reduce an idea to a reasonably abbreviated statement with the addition of several alternative answers. They can always think of myriad details about which one might wish to have information before committing himself to an answer. Such persons are better off earning a livelihood by other means. Most teachers, nonetheless, have the necessary abilities for producing effective test questions if they are sufficiently impressed with the importance of their responsibility for student appraisal to devote themselves to the task.

Rules for developing multiple-choice test items will be presented in two sections, one dealing with the item as a whole and one with the alternatives.

THE ITEM AS A WHOLE

The Direct Question vs. the Incomplete Statement

First, recall that a multiple-choice item presents a problem, either in interrogative form or as an incomplete statement, which is answered or completed in various ways. Ordinarily, the subject is to choose the one best answer to the question or the one best completion of the incomplete statement. The multiple-choice item presented earlier on page 26 was of the incomplete-statement variety, since it began,

The most essential characteristic of a psychological test is

The question might have been phrased,

What is the most essential characteristic of a psychological test?

In this illustration, the set of answers provided would serve for either form of problem. In some cases, one form or the other may require fewer words or less repetition of the same words. Economy in the use of language often governs the choice. The direct question may be preferable for subjects at a low literacy level. Some authorities seem to prefer one form or the other, some express no preference. Practically no direct experimental evidence bears upon the matter. In general, the incomplete sentence form seems to provide greater economy of language. As a rule, the item writer might best be advised to develop an item in whichever form results in the lowest reading time and least difficulty.

The Central Theme of the Item

The item as a whole should deal with a central thought. If the problem itself is not clearly presented, so that the subject has to read the answers before he knows what the question is, the item probably lacks any central theme or unity. In extreme cases, what started out to be a multiple-choice question, calling for the discrimination of different degrees of truth among alternatives, deteriorates to a cluster of true-false items, one of which clearly lies toward the true end of the continuum, while the remaining ones obviously fall toward the false end. Suppose, for example, that the item writer cuts the statement of the problem off too soon. Although he may still be attempting to produce an item dealing with the general concept that a good psychological test must adequately serve its purpose, he is very likely to produce a faulty item if he starts as follows:

A psychological test
(1) must adequately serve its purpose.

Now think of the many different ways in which a sentence beginning "A psychological test" can end. Some of the endings might constitute plausible answers to the question that the item writer had in mind, while other possible completions would answer quite different questions. Thus the item writer, who may not himself have defined his question precisely, may think of some of the following alternatives:

(2) is a device often used to predict scholarship;

(3) may be either an individual test or a group test;
(4) must be amenable to accurate scoring;
(5) is sometimes unpopular with the subjects;
(6) should yield reliable scores;
(7) should be acceptable to the subjects;
(8) should adequately cover the area concerned;
(9) is difficult to construct.

The reader can extend this list for himself. Note, now, that the completions that readily occur to one tend to have an element of truth, so that they seem to be quite reasonable fulfillments of the sentence that started "A psychological test." If one attempts to make them unacceptable as the best answers to the question by inserting some negative word, they become too obviously wrong and no longer constitute plausible alternatives.

Importance of the Ability Tested

The concept around which an idea is to be developed should be important and as closely related as possible to one of the teaching objectives. Effort should be made to base items on fundamental concepts, purposes, causal relationships, extensions of applications to new problems, and the like, rather than on facts acquired by rote memory or inconsequential details.

Clarity of Expression

The item should be expressed in precise language. This does not necessarily mean that the terminology need be highly technical, although such language is quite appropriate if its understanding is one of the objectives to be tested. Note that the illustration referred to a *psychological* test since discriminations were sought that centered around this particular kind of test rather than around the general concept of any kind of test. Of course, this narrowing of the problem also had a bearing on the choice of some of the alternatives, which were clearly related to psychological tests but would not be pertinent to other kinds of tests. Note also that the problem called for "the most essential characteristic" rather than merely "a characteristic" of a psychological test. For the latter problem, the poorer alternatives (or *distracters* as they are sometimes called) would have to be much further afield. With the item as phrased, all of the alternatives can be features of psychological tests—even fairly important ones—but the problem requires selection of the most essential one.

Brevity of Expression

Economy in the use of language, so as to reduce reading time and complexity, is one of the most important features of good test construction. It is also one of the most difficult of adoption, especially when the item writers are also teachers. Teachers have an overwhelming didactic motivation even when writing items rather than addressing a class. They feel a compulsion to tell the students something in the statement of the problem, although it may have no bearing whatever on the answer to the question. Sometimes, too, the item writer is impelled to include in the statement of the problem some justification of the importance of the concept being tested. Thus, in developing an idea into an item, he might begin by writing:

> Psychological tests have many important characteristics. Most competent authorities would agree, however, that the most essential of the following characteristics is

Or he might write:

> The item constructor should know that the most essential characteristic of a psychological test is

Or something like:

> Although psychological tests may differ in several respects, they are alike in that the most important characteristic of any such test is

Or he might become ultraconservative and say:

> Our textbook claims that the most important characteristic of a psychological test is

The question may even be needlessly complicated by including some unnecessary specificity or irrelevancy, such as the name of some obscure writer:

> Adkins claims that the most essential characteristic of a psychological test is

If the teaching has been effective, usually the concept itself is important, not the name of a particular writer who happens to have discussed it last.

Avoid Dangling Constructions

Sometimes the item writer becomes entangled in unduly complex and awkward word arrangements or in poor grammatical constructions. One of the commonest faults is the use of dangling participles or gerunds. When sentences are introduced by participles or gerunds, the subject of the principal clause must be the actor implied in the introductory verbal. The unwary item writer may produce:

> When constructing a psychological test, the most essential characteristic is

Avoid Weak Sentence Structure

Another fault frequently encountered in item writing is the unnecessary use of weak sentence structure, as exemplified by the anticipatory "it." Thus:

> It is the most essential characteristic of a psychological test that it

Much more straightforward is:

> The most essential characteristic of a psychological test is

Avoid Irrelevant Inaccuracies

Irrelevant inaccuracies either in the statement of the problem or in the alternatives are to be avoided. Thus suppose that the problem statement read:

> Adkins first stressed that the most essential characteristic of a psychological test is

Although inclusion of the inaccuracy does not alter the intended answer, the students would know that establishment of a first source of such a statement is patently impossible. Such inaccuracies in items, even though not affecting the ability of students to answer correctly, can serve only to diminish their confidence in a test.

Avoid Irrelevant Sources of Difficulty

Item writers should also avoid irrelevant sources of difficulty in test items. Unnecessary difficulty of vocabulary is a case in point. For example, if the problem read:

> The most essential characteristic of a psychometric device is

the more unusual vocabulary might make the item more difficult.

Avoid Stereotypy

Stereotyped phraseology, either in the statement of the problem or in the alternatives, places too high a premium upon mere rote memory and gives credit for correct responses to students who lack basic understanding of concepts. Suppose that the intended answer were replaced by the following:

(1) the extent to which it measures what it is supposed to measure.

This concept of test validity is classic, even though some of the more recent and perhaps more sophisticated treatments of the subject would regard it as an oversimplification. The casual student might well have recalled this as a definition of validity, and since the term *validity* is a very good-sounding one, he might well have selected this answer without having any very adequate understanding of the concept.

Include as Much as Possible in the Problem

As a general rule, the statement of the problem should include as many as possible of the words that are common to the alternatives. Exceptions to this rule are sometimes made in the case of short phrases when it seems most natural and direct to end the statement of the problem with a strong part of speech, such as a verb. Even if all the alternatives began with the same single word, such as the article *the,* reading of the item might well be facilitated by repeating this article as the first word in every alternative. Sometimes, however, recasting the statement of the problem serves to avoid needless repetition of long phrases in each alternative.

Present Items in Positive Form

As a general principle, questions should be cast in positive form. By negative items is meant those which ask what is *not* a characteristic of something, what is the *least* defensible reason for something, what is the *least* frequent occurrence, etc. The beginning item writer who finds a convenient listing of a number of characteristics may quickly produce an item by phrasing a negative question. He uses the listed elements as distracters, and himself produces one alternative that does not belong with the listed elements and that therefore will serve as the answer to the negative question. While the item is quickly produced, often the resulting correct answer is too obvious. Moreover, the negative item presents a psychological disadvantage to the subject, who naturally prefers to indicate best answers rather than unacceptable solutions.

Particularly to be avoided is entanglement with double negatives or even triple negatives. If the problem reads:

Which of the following item faults is least defensible?

and an alternative is:

Failure to avoid double negatives.

the reader can scarcely be blamed for confusion and irritation.

Emphasize Any Negative Aspect of the Problem

Nevertheless, the item writer, sometimes finding that he cannot produce a positively stated item upon some important concept, will then resort to a negative item. Since students who are set for positive items tend to misread negative ones, the negative aspect of the item should be emphasized in some way, as by underlining, italics, or upper-case letters.

THE ALTERNATIVES

Plausibility of the Alternatives

All of the alternatives should follow both plausibly and grammatically from the statement of the problem. Although one answer should be agreed upon by experts as the best of the alternatives, the intended wrong answers, too, should have an element of plausibility. If one of the distracters does not seem to some student to be a reasonable answer to the problem set, it is serving no useful purpose and should be replaced by another alternative that may seem acceptable to someone.

Lack of Parallel Structure as a Specific Determiner

The answers should be parallel in grammatical form. Each should be read with the premise or problem as a unit, as a check upon whether or not it does follow grammatically. Suppose that in our illustrative item the intended answer read:

(1) how well it serves its purpose.

The grammatical structure of this alternative is then different from that of the others. This very dissimilarity may lead the subjects to single it out for special attention and perhaps to choose it as the best answer. The lack of parallelism also may cause others, even some who initially favored the alternative, to avoid it. For the distracters, as well as for the intended answers, similar grammatical form is the best rule.

Lack of grammatical parallelism is one illustration of a larger class of item faults that goes under the general designation of *specific determiners*. A specific determiner is any extraneous clue in any part of an item —that is, some sign unrelated to actual knowledge of the subject matter that tends to lead the subject correctly to infer that a particular answer is intended as correct or as incorrect. Thus in the previous illustration the specific determiner was some grammatical difference of one alternative from all the others. The test constructor should be alert to many kinds of clues.

Particular Words as Specific Determiners

Another type of specific determiner arises from the fact that certain words, such as *always* or *never,* tend to appear in false statements. Students quickly learn to take advantage of this kind of clue. Fortunately, the writer of true-false items also usually becomes aware of this fact, but he may not realize that it is equally applicable to alternatives in multiple-choice items.

Particular words that provide undesired clues as to the rightness or wrongness of an answer abound in every subject-matter field. For example, if only one alternative for an item in the field of social work includes the notion that the problem will be "discussed," that alternative was almost certainly intended as a best answer. New item writers may have a tendency to use only very acceptable diction and concepts in the best answers; this inclination, when it persists, provides clues to the subjects. Note that in our sample item the incorrect alternatives contain good concepts—accuracy, acceptability, completeness. Such words are used intentionally in the wrong answers when words with equally favorable connotations must appear in the best answer.

Relative Length of an Alternative as a Specific Determiner

A common specific determiner lies in the length of the best answer as compared with that of the poorer ones. The item writer may be particu-

larly careful to express the best answer quite fully, with all of the qualifications that occur to him. Since he thinks of the poorer answers as incorrect, he sees no necessity for qualifications. Hence they may tend to
be shorter. In other instances, the best answer may be expressed in a very
brief yet precise phrase, while no such language occurs to the writer for
expressing wrong answers. In this case, the best answer may stand out as
the shortest one.

Some persons in the field of testing have suggested that all the answers
to a particular item should be of about the same length. Perhaps such a
rule is unnecessarily restrictive. The item writer should be cautioned,
however, not to let any particular pattern reveal itself in the relative length
of the best answer. Thus occasionally the answers will all be of the same
length, while at other times the best answer and only one or two of the
distracters may be significantly shorter than the other distracters, and so
on. If no pattern becomes apparent, undesirable clues will not intrude.

Repetition of Language as a Specific Determiner

Still another type of specific determiner appears when the best answer
repeats some of the same terms used in the statement of the problem. If
such repetition seems to be necessary, care should be taken to duplicate
some of the same language in other alternatives as well.

Vague Pronouns as Specific Determiners

The item writer commonly writes the best answer first. In writing other
answers he has a natural tendency to use pronouns for certain words that
occur in the answer that he produced first. If he reads all of the answers,
he notes no vagueness with reference to pronouns. What happens, however,
when the order of the answers is changed as the item is being readied
for a test? Some of the alternatives that appear in the first positions may
now contain pronouns which lack reference. The vagueness of their meaning will then provide the subject with a strong hint that none of them is
intended as the best answer. When he then comes to the answer that does
not have this characteristic, he at once selects it. Again, then, a specific
determiner inheres in the structure of the item. The solution is simply to
avoid in distracters the use of pronouns whose referents appear only in
the best answer. For this reason, item writing will of necessity be more
redundant than ordinary prose.

Opposite Alternatives as Specific Determiners

After a problem and a best answer have been written, a natural wrong answer may seem to be the opposite to the best answer. Ordinarily, the student who sees a pair of opposites among the alternatives for an item can tell automatically that one of the two is the intended answer. Hence his choice of answers is narrowed at once to two rather than to the four or five ostensible alternatives. If it seems likely that some students will think the opposite of the best answer is in fact the intended answer, then sometimes it can be used among the alternatives if the precaution is taken of including among the alternatives another pair of opposites neither of which is defensible as the best answer.

Technical Terms as Specific Determiners

Occasionally the item writer, seeking desperately for a distracter, incorporates a term so technical that students may recognize that they have not been exposed to it. Hence they will tend to avoid it. Possibly in some cases a highly technical word which the student has encountered but which he does not understand clearly may lead him to mark the answer that includes it. In general, such ruses should be avoided. Suppose, for example, that our sample item included as a distracter,

its tendency towards homoscedasticity.

Probably not many subjects would select this answer. Unless the test as a whole deals with a highly technical vocabulary, such a term serves merely as an unwarranted clue.

Overlapping Alternatives as Specific Determiners

Still another type of specific determiner arises when one response over-laps or includes one or more other alternatives. In such a case, the subject knows that if the one response is correct, the additional overlapping ones must also be correct. Since he has been instructed to select only one answer, this type of clue may enable him to discard all of the overlapping choices and narrow his decision to alternatives that do not have this characteristic. In other instances, if one of the overlapping choices is intended as the correct answer, the subject can argue legitimately that other answers must also be correct. This type of defect is seen most frequently in items with numerical answers. Thus if the best answer to an item is intended to be

less than 10%

similarly structured alternatives with percentages higher than ten must automatically be correct. Once the item writer becomes aware of this typ of defect, he can avoid it by various devices.

Synonymous Distracters as Specific Determiners

Another similar type of trouble ensues when one alternative mea essentially the same as another alternative. This would obviously cause difficulty if the best answer were one of the two alternatives in question. The problem is more subtle and also more frequent in the case of two wrong alternatives. The item writer, hard-pressed for an idea for a distracter, may see no harm in re-expressing in different language an idea that has already been used. But the subject may well realize that if one of the answers were correct the second would also have to be correct. Since he has been instructed to select only one answer, he narrows his range of choice to the other alternatives. These synonymous distracters operate as specific determiners.

Use of "None of the Above" and "All of the Above"

Sooner or later, item writers learn about the possibility of using "none of these" (or "none of the above") or "all of the above" as the last alternative for an item. "None of the above" is of course used when none of the alternatives presented earlier is correct, while "all of the above" can be the answer when all of the alternatives are correct. When such alternatives are used, they must constitute the correct answers in an appropriate proportion of items.

Cautiously used, these devices have merit in special situations. They create a problem, however, when the item writer resorts to them as a substitute for thought. Thus when he lacks an inspiration for the last needed alternative, he suddenly may achieve closure by writing "none of these." The result may be that this alternative is used inappropriately. "None of the above" is never properly included among the alternatives of an item intended to test the discrimination among alternatives of various degrees of goodness. It should be used only when each alternative can be rated unambiguously as correct or incorrect. Thus it is more appropriate for items testing factual knowledge than for those involving any discriminative judgment.

The use of "none of the above" partakes of some of the disadvantages of negative items, that is, items that tend to require the subject to select an answer which is *not* an answer, in a sense. Ordinarily, the subject approaching a test item is posed a problem to which he seeks a positive answer. A tentative response may occur to him, and he may seek the nearest equivalent among the answers presented. In case "none of the above" is the intended answer to a question, however, he seeks in vain for an opportunity to demonstrate positively that he can select the best solution, and he may feel deflated when the only indication of his knowledge that he can offer is to mark "none of the above."

The use of "none of these" as an alternative seems to be most defensible in the case of problems that require numerical computations when these must be presented in multiple-choice form. One could well argue that such items could better be presented in completion form, since the marking can be quite objective. Occasionally, however, computational problems are to be included in a test containing other types of multiple-choice items, and having all of the items in the same form may well be a matter of great convenience. When computational items are presented in the multiple-choice form, anticipation of the errors that the unknowing subjects will make is often difficult, and the number of likely errors may be so great that not all of them can be represented among the alternatives. When this happens, the subject who makes an error not represented by one of the alternatives automatically knows that his solution is incorrect. He may continue working until he hits upon the correct solution, which often may be among the alternatives. "None of these" can be used most appropriately as the correct answer for items in which the likely errors are relatively few and can thus be represented among the other alternatives.

Use of "all of the above" has even less to recommend it. Consider, for example, a five-choice item in which "all of the above," the fifth choice, is the intended answer. Now if the subject realizes that any two of the preceding four alternatives are correct, he automatically knows that "all of the above" is the answer. To resort frankly to a series of true-false questions is better than to use "all of the above" as one of the alternatives in multiple-choice questions.

Either "none of the above" or "all of the above" as an alternative for the illustrative item that we have been using would be clearly inappropriate. The novice at item writing, however, may find in some written source material a list of several characteristics, advantages, arguments, and so on. He quickly produces an item by using the listing to provide his first alternatives and uses "all of the above" as the answer. Such an item ordinarily is subject to improvement.

Compound Responses

Special mention should be made of a type of alternative that represents a compound response. Such responses may present, for example, both a what and a why, or both a person and a situation. Some writers have even recommended such compound responses as a means of controlling the difficulty of the item. Thus, it has been argued, the item may be simplified by permitting the subject to select an answer either on the basis of the who or on the basis of the what; or the difficulty can be increased by requiring the subject to demonstrate two abilities in choosing his answer. Let us examine such an item:

> When the length of an objective test is reduced by discarding one-half of its items at random, what would be expected to happen to its validity? Why?
> (1) It would decrease due to a reduction in content reliability.
> (2) It would remain unchanged because the retained items would be as valid as the discarded ones.
> (3) It would increase because the subjects would not be so fatigued by an equally good test half as long.
> (4) It would decrease due to a reduction in scoring reliability.
> (5) It would increase due to an increase in temporal stability of the resulting scores.

The intention of the item writer was that the score would be one for a correct answer and zero for an incorrect answer. Yet the score of one presents an ambiguity of interpretation. It may mean that the subject knew only what happened, only why something happened, or both what happened and why it happened. Preferably, the item could be divided into two items and the ambiguity completely avoided. The items might read as follows:

> When the length of an objective test having a validity coefficient of .50 is reduced by discarding one-half of its items at random, its validity would be expected to
> (1) decrease some;
> (2) decrease to nearly zero;

(3) increase some;
(4) increase to nearly 1.00;
(5) remain unchanged.
When the length of an objective test is reduced by discarding some items at random, the resulting effect upon its validity would be attributable to
(1) decrease in content reliability;
(2) the equal validity of the retained and discarded items;
(3) a reduction in the effect of fatigue;
(4) decrease in scoring reliability;
(5) increase in temporal reliability.

Note now that the student who knows both the effect and the reason for it will receive a total score of two. The student who knows one of these facts but not the other will receive a score of one, and the student who knows neither will receive a score of zero. Here the score on each item is unambiguous and the final score for each student better reflects his degree of knowledge.

INDEPENDENCE OF ITEMS IN A TEST

As a general rule, each item in a test should be independent of other items. Attention to this matter of the possible overlapping of items becomes uppermost at the time items are being assembled into a test. The test constructor working on individual items, however, should also keep in mind the possibility that one item may overlap another in an undesirable way; thus he can eliminate from his items at the point of construction terms or phrases that would probably cause them to overlap. Such attention has the additional advantage that it tends to reduce unnecessary verbiage. Keeping records on the use of items and on some of their statistical characteristics becomes complicated when the wording of the item must be changed to avoid its giving away the answer to another item. For this reason, individual items should be as trim as possible in the first instance so that not many of them will need to be altered to avoid overlapping.

When items are being selected from a file to comprise a test, the same question may appear in different guises. Such overlapping is avoided best not by altering one item but simply by omitting it. The other type of overlapping, in which the answer to one item is made clear by something contained in another item, even though it does not present the same question, is more subtle and requires greater alertness to detect.

Recall our sample item:

The most essential characteristic of a psychological test is
(1) the adequacy with which it serves its purpose;
(2) etc.

Now suppose that our item file contains another problem that reads in part as follows:

The extent to which a test serves its purpose is known as its
(1) validity;
(2) etc.

Since the word "validity" has such a noble sound, the student may at once argue that validity must be the most essential characteristic of a psychological test. Hence, if a student knows that the extent to which a test serves its purpose is called validity, he must also know that the most essential characteristic of a psychological test is the adequacy with which it serves its purpose. Thus in this case the undesirable overlapping comes from the overlapping of the premise of one problem with the answer of another.

POSITION OF THE BEST ANSWER

Random Placement of the Alternatives

The item writer should first construct the statement of the problem and then, in the initial draft of an item, place the best or intended answer in the first position among the alternatives. Usually the item writer should not decide by an act of judgment in which position to place the best answer in the final version of the item. The reason for this prohibition is that the item writer is likely to have unconscious biases that will influence the positions he assigns. Many persons would tend to use the third position too often for the answer in five-choice items and to under-use the first position and, perhaps to a lesser extent, the fifth position. If the biases of a subject happen to agree with those of the constructor, or if the subject gets a hunch to the effect that, say, the first answer presented is rarely the intended answer or that, other things equal, the third answer is his best guess, he will get too high a score.

For items with a particular number of choices, say five, a listing of all the possible orders of the alternatives can be made readily. A section of such a table might appear as follows:

1. A B C D E
2. B A C D E
3. C A B D E
4. D A B C E
5. E A B C D
6. A C B D E
7. B C A D E

In the preparation of such a table, one can readily adopt some systematic scheme for setting down all possible orders. If the table is likely to be used for a relatively small number of items at a time, the letters appearing in the first position should be altered systematically, as in the illustration above. In using the table, one would assign position A (or the first position) to the first alternative for the first item, position B for the second alternative for this item, and so on. For the second item being processed, he would assign position B (or the second position) to the first alternative, position A (or the first position) to the second alternative, and so on. For the third item, position C (or the third position) is assigned to the first alternative written and hence to the best answer.

If a large number of items are to have their alternatives randomized, a clerk can simply apply the positions indicated in the table to the alternatives in each item in turn, recording next to each alternative a letter to indicate the position in which it is to be typed. A simpler procedure in some instances might be to use letters to identify the alternatives in the initial draft of the items and then to compose the table of alternative positions in terms of the numbers from one to five rather than in terms of the letters A to E. The clerk applying such a table makes a note of the last order used for a particular set of items and starts with the next order when applying the table to a new set of items. Such a scheme results in the use of all answer positions an equal number of times. When items so treated are filed and tests are later assembled from them, certain answer positions may be used by chance a significantly greater number of times than others. Ordinarily the departure from approximately equal numbers of each position is not so great as to require any special adjustment, however.

Desirable Exceptions to Randomization of Alternatives

Although the random assignment of answer positions for all alternatives is recommended in the case of most items, an exception should be made whenever the answers can be placed into a numerical sequence or into some logical order. Thus, if the alternatives for an item are 1952, 1893, 1929, 1492, and 1610, little is to be gained by requiring the subject to leap hither and yon in history. The alternatives can be placed in order of either ascending or descending size.

Other special instances will arise in which the item constructor should specify the order of the alternatives rather than leaving it to chance. If two optional answers are very similar but differ in a few words, they may well be placed next to each other in order to minimize reading difficulty and to facilitate the contrast between them. Likewise, if the alternatives contain two pairs of opposites, the members of each pair should appear together to avoid confusing the subject unnecessarily.

GAUGING ITEM DIFFICULTY

The item constructor must attempt to adjust the difficulty of the item to the subjects for whom it is intended. At this point his insight into the previous background and mental processes of his subjects will be helpful. The naive item writer may suppose that the difficulty of an item is at once apparent from the statement of the problem, but this is by no means the case. The difficulty of a particular item is a function not only of the question posed, but also of the degree of discrimination elicited by the alternatives presented.

Consider again our illustrative problem. The item should prove to be considerably simpler if it reads as follows:

> The most essential characteristic of a psychological test is
> (1) the adequacy with which it serves its purpose;
> (2) the favorable impression made by its appearance;
> (3) the extent to which it amuses the subjects;
> (4) the extent to which it resembles other familiar tests;
> (5) the susceptibility to machine-scoring.

Since the distracters are now further afield, so to speak, more students should be able to select the intended answer.

Chapter 8

Treatment of Test Scores

THE FREQUENCY DISTRIBUTION

Once an objective test has been scored, the arrangement of scores in order from high to low helps to picture how the test is working. Although the answer sheets themselves may be ordered according to score, this procedure is not necessary. The first step in making a systematic arrangement of the scores is to tally the frequencies corresponding to each. A list of all possible scores may be made on a sheet of ruled paper, usually with the highest score at the top and the lowest score at the bottom. Then a tally mark is made in the row corresponding to each particular score. If the number of tallies in some rows is too large for ready interpretation, those in each row may be added and recorded in a single column. Sometimes the symbol X is used to stand for the *variable* or the test score and the symbol f for the *frequency* with which a score occurs. An illustration of such a *frequency distribution* follows on the next page. (The reader may ignore the last column for the moment.)

THE RANGE

The difference between the highest and the lowest score (sometimes augmented by 1) indicates the spread or variability of the scores. In fact,

61

the *range* is a crude measure of variability. It is crude because, when the number of cases is small, it tends to fluctuate appreciably from one sample to another, depending upon the range of talent that happens to be included in the sample groups. Despite its sampling unreliability, the range will usually suffice as a measure of the variability of a teacher-made test when data on only a small group of subjects are available.

Score (X)	Tallies	Frequency (f)	Letter Grade
27	I	1	A+
26		0	
25	I	1	A
24	I	1	A−
23	II	2	B+
22	I	1	B
21		0	
20	II	2	B−
19	I	1	C+
18	I	1	C+
17	I	1	C
16	II	2	C
15	I	1	C−
14	I	1	C−
13		0	
12	II	2	D
11		0	
10	II	2	F+
9		0	
8		0	
7		0	
6		0	
5	I	1	F−
$n=$	20	20	

THE GROUPED FREQUENCY DISTRIBUTION

If the range of scores covers more than twenty-five points or so, some condensation of the frequency distribution is in order. This is effected by *grouping* nearby scores together and thereafter treating them as equal. Thus, in the case of the foregoing distribution, the scores may be grouped by a *class interval* of two, with the scores of 4 and 5 grouped together, 6 and 7 together, and so on. The resulting condensed or *grouped frequency distribution* would appear as in the first two columns of the illustration on the following page.

Note that the number of different scores grouped together is known as the class interval. The first interval starts conventionally with a multiple of the class interval. Usually, if grouping results in fewer than about ten class intervals, it is abandoned and an interval of one is used as in the original data.

ORIGINAL SCORES X	f	CODED SCORES X'	Xf	X'f
26-27	1	11	26.5	11
24-25	2	10	49.0	20
22-23	3	9	67.5	27
20-21	2	8	41.0	16
18-19	2	7	37.0	14
16-17	3	6	49.5	18
14-15	2	5	29.0	10
12-13	2	4	25.0	8
10-11	2	3	21.0	6
8- 9	0	2		0
6- 7	0	1		0
4- 5	1	0	4.5	0
	$n = 20$	$\Sigma X =$	350.0	$\Sigma X' = 130$

$$\text{Raw Score Mean} = \overline{X} = \frac{350.0}{20} = 17.5$$

$$\text{Coded Score Mean} = \overline{X'} = \frac{130}{20} = 6.5$$

$$\text{Decoded Mean} = \text{Raw Mean} = 2(6.5) + 4.5 = 17.5$$

Both the lower and the upper limit of each class interval are recorded, thus minimizing the possibility of errors in tallying scores.

As a partial check on one aspect of the procedure, the tally marks or the row sums should be added to ensure that the appropriate number of marks has been made.

For some purposes, all of the scores in any one interval are treated as if they fell at its midpoint. The most tenable assumption and the one most commonly made is that a particular numerical score, say 19, represents a small range of scores that might have been recorded had the unit of measurement been sufficiently fine. This range can best be regarded as extending from one-half a unit below the recorded value to one-half a unit above it. Thus a score recorded as 19 is thought of as the midpoint of an interval of possible scores ranging from 18.5 up to 19.5; 19.0 is the midpoint of this interval. Hence scores recorded at 19 are treated as if they were 19.0, consistently with the foregoing discussion.

Now with a class interval of two, as in our illustration, the theoretical or "real" range of the scores recorded in the interval labeled 4-5 is regarded as 3.5-5.5. The limits of the next interval would be regarded as 5.5-7.5, and so on. The midpoint of the lowest interval would be regarded as 4.5, that of the next higher interval as 6.5, and so on. Such midpoints can always be obtained by adding one-half of the size of the class interval to the lower limit of the class interval. Thus 3.5 plus 2/2 equals 4.5, the midpoint of the first interval.

That the midpoint turns out to be fractional whenever the class interval is an even number is troublesome to some persons. This problem can be avoided whenever it is appropriate to use an odd number for the class interval. In some situations, however, intervals that are even numbers cannot be avoided. Perhaps the most frequently used intervals are 1, 2, 3, 5, and 10, the latter two arising from deeply ingrained habits pertaining to our number system.

The process of making a frequency distribution has already yielded a measure of the *variability* of the scores. Although the range is admittedly crude, it will serve many of the purposes of the teacher. In most instances, the teacher will have no need for a stabler measure of *dispersion,* such as the *standard deviation,* which is more time-consuming to compute.

THE MEDIAN

In addition to a measure of the spread of the scores, the teacher will almost certainly want some kind of *average,* some measure of the *central tendency* of the scores. Although the *arithmetic mean* (or arithmetic average) is very simple to compute, the *median* is even simpler, especially when there is no necessity for a high degree of accuracy.

The median is the measure that is here recommended for general use with classroom tests. By definition, the median is that point along the score continuum above which and below which half of the cases fall. It is that point which divides the subjects into two equal groups. In the foregoing illustration of an ungrouped frequency distribution, the point is sought below which and above which ten cases lie. This point is reached either by counting up ten cases into the distribution from the bottom or by counting ten cases down from the top. In this case, ten subjects have scores of 18 or above and ten have scores of 17 or below. The median, then, is taken as half-way between 17 and 18. It can also be regarded as falling at the upper limit of the score labeled 17 or at the lower limit of the score labeled 18. In either case, it is 17.5. For this 33-item test, then, the median is just slightly above 50 per cent of the total number of items in the test, which is about where it should be for a typical test expected to discriminate all along the range of ability. For this illustration, the same median results from counting up ten cases in the grouped frequency distribution, but this would not necessarily be the case.

Now, considering the grouped distribution, suppose that there had been only two cases falling in the interval 16-17 and three cases in the interval 18-19. Then, as frequencies are added from the bottom up, only nine cases fall below the interval 18-19 and the tenth case falls within the interval 18-19. From the top downward are eight cases above the interval 20-21 and three more cases in the interval 18-19. Thus the tenth case from the top falls somewhere in the interval 18-19. Since there are three cases in the interval, it can be regarded as falling two-thirds of the way into the interval. Likewise, counting up from the bottom, the tenth case can be regarded as going to one-third of the distance from the bottom of the same interval. For a rough idea, which in general will suffice, the median is equal to "about 18." Greater precision comes from interpolating an appropriate distance into the interval and adding the resulting distance to the lower limit of the interval. The lower limit of the interval in which the median falls is 17.5. To this lower limit is added one-third of the two units which constitute the distance from the lower limit to the upper limit of the interval, or one-third times two. The median is thus 18.17 or, rounded, 18.2. To check, an appropriate amount is subtracted from the upper limit of the interval 19.5. Now subtracting two-thirds of the distance, represented by two units, or 1.33, again gives 18.2.

A median based upon a small number of cases tends to fluctuate appreciably from one sample to another. It is not a highly dependable statistic. Unless one wishes to report a median to his learned colleagues, the degree of accuracy illustrated above is not necessary for classroom tests in view of the generally rather small number of cases and the purposes to be served. Hence the general approach recommended is simply to count upwards halfway into the distribution and to estimate the score point which corresponds. If there were an odd number of cases in the distribution, such as twenty-one, one would then look for the eleventh case and try to guess the score point that corresponds to it.

THE ARITHMETIC MEAN

The teacher who wishes to do more statistical work with the scores in a distribution can calculate an *arithmetic mean* and perhaps a standard deviation, and possibly indices of their sampling variability. A good estimate of the mean can be obtained by multiplying the successive midpoints of the intervals by their corresponding frequencies, adding these products, and dividing by the number of cases. Or, if the numbers representing the scores are large, the frequencies can be multiplied by a set of coded scores, comprised of successive integers starting with zero for the lowest class interval, the products of the frequencies by the coded scores added, and that sum of products divided by the number of cases. Then the answer must essentially be decoded by multiplying it by the size of the class interval and adding the midpoint of the lowest class interval. This is neither difficult nor very laborious, but it is clearly more time-consuming than is a rough estimation of the median that ordinarily suffices.

For those who are interested in the computation of the mean using both uncoded and coded scores, an illustration is given. (See page 63.)

The formula for the mean can be written as:

$$\text{Raw score mean} = \overline{X} = \frac{\Sigma X}{n}$$

where the Greek letter Σ stands for the operation of addition, thus implying that all of the raw scores are to be added. In the illustration, the sum of the X's is 350.0, which, divided by n, yields a raw score mean of 17.5. That this happens to coincide with the median for this distribution is accidental. Usually the mean and the median, except for a theoretical symmetrical distribution, do not agree exactly.

The formula for decoding the coded score mean, $\overline{X}'$, can be written as follows:

$$\text{Decoded mean} = i \frac{\Sigma X'}{n} + F_o$$

where the symbol i stands for the size of the class interval and F_o stands for the face value or midpoint of the lowest class interval, that is, the one corresponding to a coded score of 0.

Observe that the numbers involved in the computation using the coded or X' scores are smaller than those using the midpoints along the original scale. For one who is reasonably adept with a calculating machine, the products of the score values times frequencies need not be recorded but can be cumulated directly on the machine.

OTHER MEASURES OF DISPERSION

If for any reason the teacher wishes a more refined measure of dispersion than the range, he might look into the *semi-interquartile range*, as a measure frequently recommended along with the median, and the standard deviation, as the measure that typically accompanies the arithmetic mean. Descriptions of these measures and the corresponding computational procedures are so common in elementary statistics texts that they will not be repeated here. Nor will any treatment of the sampling errors of these statistics need to be offered.

TRANSLATING RAW SCORES TO LETTER GRADES

Once the frequency distribution is available, together with a measure of dispersion and central tendency, the question arises of interpreting different scores on the tests. Perhaps most typically the teacher finds it necessary to translate numerical scores into letter-grade equivalents, since most final course marks are recorded in terms of letters, such as A, B, C, D, and E or F. Because percentage scales are quite arbitrary, the conversion of numerical grades into percentage terms and the application of some fixed translation scheme make no sense whatever. Thus the statements that continue to clutter up pre-college grading regulations and college catalogues, to the effect that a grade range of, say, 91-100 corresponds to A, 86-90 to B, and so on, have no justification whatever. If the 0 and 100 points have no significance, obviously neither do any other selected points, such as 70 or 60, which are often cited as minimal passing grades. This outmoded insistence upon the use of fixed tables of equivalents for interpreting scores is largely responsible for the fact that tests tend to be too easy to be optimally discriminating.

The only sound course is to recognize from the start that the concentration of the frequencies of scores and the relative dispersion of scores are functions of the average difficulty of the items, the range of difficulty of the items, and the interrelationships among the items. The distribution used in the foregoing illustrations is an actual distribution of scores on a thirty-three-item test used in a course in elementary psychological statistics, a course taken by fifteen juniors and seniors and five graduate students. If one should apply the standard that 70 per cent of the items constitutes a minimally passing score, then five of these students would pass and fifteen would fail. Such a dilemma could always be avoided by giving a much easier test, but it would tell less about the differences among the students. The preferable procedure is to attempt to control the difficulty of the test so that the average score will be about 50 per cent of the items and then to recognize clearly that some judgment must be applied in attempting to set letter-grade equivalents.

If one must have fixed rules for establishing letter grades, setting them in terms of percentages of the different ones to be assigned is far better than reliance upon arbitrary raw-score equivalents for the different letter grades. A teacher should not expect to adhere rigorously to any fixed percentages of the different letter grades for every test that is given. Rather, he should have in mind some general standard which his letter-grade equivalents would tend toward over a period of perhaps several years. Such a standard should be followed more strictly for very large classes than for some particular small class, in which the students may be atypically good or poor.

Schools and colleges should do more toward setting up what they regard to be general standards for the percentages of different letter grades for courses at different levels. These would be regarded as guidelines rather than as absolute standards to be applied for every course. Certainly to be taken into account, as in the current example, should be the percentages of students at different levels who are taking a course.

The particular letter-grade equivalents that were assigned for the illustrative test are shown in the first illustration of the frequency distribution (p. 62). The pluses and minuses were assigned because of a wish to take into account later whether a particular letter grade fell high in the range or low in the range, so that they could have different effects on the final average mark. The C range extends further below the median than it does above, because of the number of graduate students in the class. Also, since this was a class for upperclassmen and graduate students rather than for freshmen and sophomores, no necessity to adhere to a normal or symmetrical distribution of letter-grade equivalents was felt.

APPLICATION OF SUGGESTED GUIDE DISTRIBUTIONS

A college teacher might find it useful to attempt to apply roughly the following distributions of letter grades to separate fifty-minute quizzes for freshman-sophomore and for junior-senior classes, respectively:

	Freshman-Sophomore	Junior-Senior
A	9	12
B	26	28
C	30	44
D	26	12
F	9	4

A pre-college teacher might find the first distribution generally serviceable.

These distributions have relatively larger percentages of A's and B's as well as of D's and F's than would be applicable in the assignment of final grades to be based on averages of the quizzes and final examination. The reason for this is that scores based on averages tend to regress toward the mean when there is less than perfect correlation between the measures averaged. The student who gets an A on the first quiz, if he fails to get an A on the second, will not get a mark higher than A but rather one lower. Thus the distribution of average letter grades, all based upon the same distribution scheme, will always be more peaked or have fewer cases at the extremes. Without some special precautionary measures, one could well find that the average grades assigned are restricted to D's, C's and B's, with no students averaging F and none A. Some teachers avoid this dilemma by refusing to provide letter-grade equivalents for scores on the separate components of the final grade. Students complain, however, that they then lack knowledge of how they stand, and their motivation may become progressively worse. For this reason, many teachers rather blindly assign letter grades on each separate measure with no very clear notion as to what is likely to result when these are averaged.

At this point, a word is in order as to why the suggested guide distributions for individual quizzes for the two groups differ. A reasonable supposition is that many of the D and F students at the freshman-sophomore level will not have survived to the junior-senior level. Hence their performance is under-represented in the raw-score distributions for the test given to upperclassmen. Correction for this selective drop-out seems clearly to be in order. One might expect small increases in percentages of A's and B's at the upperclass level, a marked decrease in D's and F's, and a sharp increase in C's. The guide distributions should reflect such expectations.

COMBINING LETTER GRADES FROM
SEVERAL EXAMINATIONS

If distributions essentially like the foregoing are used for the individual quizzes and the final examination, then some appropriately weighted averages of the letter grades on these separate examinations could be expected to have some such distributions as the following:

	Freshman-Sophomore	Junior-Senior
A	6	7
B	25	29
C	38	55
D	25	7
F	6	2

The first of these distributions would yield frequencies approximating those of the *normal distribution,* which is symmetrical and bell-shaped, whereas the second has slightly more A's and B's, many more C's, and significantly fewer D's and F's. These differences between the two distributions seem appropriate in view of the selective factors referred to above. These distributions of final grades have not been derived mathematically from the earlier ones. Their exact character will depend upon the degree of relationship among the sets of grades to be combined and the number to be combined. The author's experience leads to a belief that they represent reasonable expectations when four or five sets of letter grades, intercorrelated with each other to the extent of about .30 to .75, are combined.

The following table will illustrate the kind of results that might be expected. It presents hypothetical letter-grade assignments on four measures, three fifty-minute quizzes and a two-hour final, to be combined with the quizzes at double weight. Each distribution of letter grades for the twenty-five students contains 2 A's, 7 B's, 8 C's, 6 D's and 2 F's. This is as close as possible to the originally suggested percentage distribution on individual quizzes for freshmen and sophomores—9 per cent, 26 per cent, 30 per cent, 26 per cent, and 9 per cent. The simplest way to get the average letter grade for each student is to translate into numerical terms as follows: A = 4, B = 3, C = 2, D = 1, F = 0. Performing this translation mentally and adding, with the number corresponding to the final examination being multiplied by two, we get the total number of points

for each student. These can be converted into averages by dividing each
by five or multiplying by .2. Then the averages can be readily converted

	QUIZ 1	QUIZ 2	QUIZ 3	Final*	Total Points	Average Points	Final Grade
1	A	B	B	A	18	3.6	A
2	A	B	B	A	18	3.6	A
3	B	A	B	C	14	2.8	B
4	B	B	C	B	14	2.8	B
5	B	B	C	B	14	2.8	B
6	B	D	A	B	13	2.6	B
7	B	C	B	B	14	2.8	B
8	B	C	C	C	9	1.8	C
9	B	D	C	B	12	2.4	C
10	C	A	A	B	16	3.2	B
11	C	B	C	C	11	2.2	C
12	C	B	D	C	10	2.0	C
13	C	D	D	C	8	1.6	C
14	C	D	B	C	10	2.0	C
15	C	C	B	D	9	1.8	C
16	C	C	F	D	6	1.2	D
17	C	F	C	C	8	1.6	C
18	D	C	B	B	12	2.4	C
19	D	B	C	D	8	1.6	C
20	D	C	D	D	6	1.2	D
21	D	C	D	F	4	.8	D
22	D	D	C	D	6	1.2	D
23	D	F	F	F	1	.2	F
24	F	D	C	D	5	1.0	D
25	F	C	D	C	7	1.4	D

*weighted double

back to letter grades, 3.5 to 4.0 being equated with A, 2.5 to 3.5 with B,
1.5 to 2.5 with C, .5 to 1.5 with D, and 0 to .5 with F. Now the frequency
distribution of these final letter grades is as follows:

Letter grade	f
A	2
B	6
C	10
D	6
F	1
	$n = 25$

This corresponds very closely to the suggested percentage distribution for
final grades for the freshman-sophomore level.

The teacher may add a degree of refinement to the processing of letter
grades by assigning pluses and minuses to them, as illustrated in the

frequency distribution on page 62. Then the averages can be computed by assigning 14 points to A+, 13 to A, 12 to A—, 11 to B+, 10 to B, and so on down to 1 for F and 0 for F—. This gives some advantage to the student who gets a high C, for example, and a disadvantage to the one who gets a low C. Final letter grades can be computed as before. A student who received grades of B, D, C on the three quizzes and B+ on the final examination (weighted double) would receive average points equivalent to a B— if the plus value in the final is taken into account. Hence his final grade would be B. Without regard to the plus value on the final, his average grade would be a high C and his final grade would be simply C. Students usually regard the procedure of assigning plus and minus values as eminently fair, and it doubtless contributes to the validity of the final grades.

FURTHER CONSIDERATIONS IN COMBINING MEASURES

One important feature of the procedures for converting grades that are recommended here is that they have the effect of transforming the frequency distribution of each test to essentially the same form before the tests are combined. Thus the teacher can compensate for tests that may be unusually difficult or unusually easy. Perhaps even more important, if all of the measures to be combined have about equal variability, their actual effects are much more likely to correspond to the intent of the teacher than if the variabilities of the measures differ substantially. In the simplest case, where just two sets of measures are to be combined, if the variability of one set is twice that of the other, it contributes substantially more to the variability of the total scores. Thus the real effects or weights of the two variables are not equal, even though they may appear to be combined at equal weights. True, the test with greater variability may be more reliable and thus should have more weight. But if the difference in variability is more probably attributable to the arbitrary nature of different units of measurement in the two cases, then some corrective procedure is in order.

The total procedure for assigning letter grades described above, following guide distributions, will essentially convert each test to the same scale. Thus each set of letter-grade equivalents will have the same general frequency distribution before the tests are combined. Then if one test is more reliable or seems more important than others (as in the case of the final examination in the example), that test can be multiplied by the desired weight (two in the example). With such treatment of data, tests are much more likely to be appropriately weighted than would be the case if numerical grades were simply added. Moreover, at any time during a course, a student can compute his to-date letter-grade standing and be reasonably confident that he has a realistic estimate of his standing in the teacher's book.

The question of how the apparent or intended weights that a teacher may wish to assign to different tests may differ from their real or actual weights is somewhat technical. No attempt will be made to treat it fully here, but the teacher should have some understanding of the problem.

Surprisingly, the mean score of a test (or any other measure of central tendency) has nothing whatever to do with its weight. Below are several sets of scores for just five students.

TESTS

STUDENT	X_1	X_2	X_3	$X_1 + X_2$	$X_1 + X_{2/2}$	$X_1 + X_3$
A	10	40	40	50	30	50
B	15	50	40	65	40	55
C	20	30	40	50	35	60
D	25	20	40	45	35	65
E	30	60	40	90	60	70

Note first that the means of Tests 2 and 3 are both 40. Then observe that the range of Test 2 is twice that of Test 1, while the scores of Test 3 do not vary at all. Now when Tests 1 and 2 are simply added, Test 2 has considerably more weight—not because its mean is twice the mean of Test 1 but rather because its range (or variability) is twice that of Test 1. If it were the intent to give them equal weight, the scores of Test 2 could be divided by 2 (or those of Test 1 multiplied by 2) in order to equate their ranges before they are combined. No correction is needed to equate the means, because they have nothing whatever to do with the relative scores and hence with the individual difference among the students when the two tests are combined.

Now Test 3, with no variability at all, when combined with Test 1 or Test 2, merely has the effect of adding a constant amount to each student's score. It yields no information about individual differences and makes no contribution to the variability of the composite score. The relative positions of the students and the numerical distances separating them are exactly the same as for Test 1 or Test 2 alone. Hence nothing is gained by adding Test 3.

When several tests are combined, then, those with greater variability have greater weight. These generalizations grow from the formula for the variance of a sum of measures, which contains not only the variances of the individual measures but also the products of the standard deviations and intercorrelation coefficients of the different pairs of measures.[1]

Occasions may arise when it will be desirable to correct unintentional weighting by multiplication or division of certain scores by appropriate constants. At other times, the problem can be obviated at once in the assignment of letter grades that are to be combined with other letter grades.

AN ALTERNATIVE PROCEDURE FOR
COMBINING SCORES

Some teachers argue for an alternative procedure in combining separate examinations in a course. They point out that the division of the total number of items presented in all the tests into separate tests is arbitrary and that all of the items should be treated at the end as if they comprised just one long test. Hence raw scores on the separate tests, they argue, can be added together at the end of the course, perhaps with the number of points on the final examination multiplied by some arbitrary constant such as two or three to give it more weight. Then letter-grade equivalents are assigned on the basis of inspection of the frequency distribution of total scores.

This procedure can be defended on logical grounds. Its most serious drawback is that students want to know how they stand on each separate quiz. If the teacher assigns letter-grade equivalents for the separate quizzes, he is likely to transform the shape of the distribution, in effect. The most likely result will be that at the end of the course the student's final letter-grade standing, based on the distribution of total points, is not perfectly related to the average of letter-grade standings previously assigned for the individual tests. Naturally, such a situation is disgruntling to the students.

---

[1]See, for example, Dorothy C. Adkins *et al, Construction and Analysis of Achievement Tests* (Washington, D. C.: U. S. Civil Service Commission, 1947), p. 192. The teacher is usually safe in ignoring the additional complicating factor arising from the fact that the higher the correlation of one test with the others, the greater will be its effective weight.

The procedure recommended earlier, calling for transformation of each set of test grades into letter-grade equivalents and later combining them at announced weights, obviates this problem. It is also more likely to result in weights for the several components of the final grade that are closer to the actual intent of the teacher.

ANOTHER EXAMPLE OF PROBLEMS IN
COMBINING SCORES

The following table will illustrate another kind of problem the teacher may encounter when he assigns letter-grade equivalents to each of several tests, then later combines the tests at whatever weights he may have announced (such as equal weights for the fifty-minute tests and double weight for the final). The table shows raw scores on four tests, three fifty-minute tests and one two-hour final. The first test had thirty items and a range of fifteen. The second test had sixty shorter items and a range of thirty-seven. The third, a test with thirty-five items, had a range of thirteen, while the 100-item final had a range of sixty-one. Using the variability as a rough indicator of the weights, the first and third tests, if simply added together, would have about the same weights. The second would have well over twice the weight of the first and third, and the final well over four times their weight. If the teacher does not take into account the differing variabilities of the tests and decides to multiply the final examination score by two before combining it with the others, he will get the composite scores in column 10. He might then assign letter grades as in column 11. Now when the student tries to verify his own standing from his letter-grade equivalents on the several tests, weighting the final twice as heavily as the others, he would reach first the average number of points shown in column 12 and then the converted letter grades of column 13.

But note that in four cases (40 per cent of the group), the letter grades the students reach differ from those assigned by the teacher—not a happy state of affairs, especially for the three who will be convinced that their grades should be higher.

Observe, however, what would happen if the teacher were to make some rough corrections for the differences in ranges and hence for the unintentional differences in the weights of the variables being combined.

	1ST TEST 30 ITEMS		2ND TEST 60 ITEMS		3RD TEST 35 ITEMS		FINAL TEST 100 ITEMS		WEIGHTED* AVERAGES		WEIGHTED† AVERAGES LETTER-GRADE EQUIVALENTS		WEIGHTED‡ AVERAGES WITH EQUATED RANGE	
1 PERSON	2 Raw Score	3 Letter Grade	4 Raw Score	5 Letter Grade	6 Raw Score	7 Letter Grade	8 Raw Score	9 Letter Grade	10 Raw Score	11 Letter Grade	12 Points	13 Letter Grade	14 Points	15 Letter Grade
1	27	A	47	A	28	A	82	B	266	B	3.6	A	267	A
2	23	B	55	A	29	A	89	A	285	A	3.8	A	277	A
3	19	C	45	B	30	A	88	A	270	A	3.4	B	261	B
4	19	C	42	C	19	D	73	B	226	C	2.2	C	210	C
5	17	C	33	C	26	B	55	C	186	C	2.2	C	210	C
6	15	C	28	C	24	C	57	C	181	C	2.0	C	197	C
7	14	D	27	C	20	D	28	F	117	F	.8	D	143	D
8	14	D	18	F	17	F	43	C	135	D	1.0	D	140	D
9	12	F	18	F	17	F	34	D	115	F	.4	F	127	F
10	25	A	23	D	21	C	38	D	145	D	1.8	C	174	C

*Obtained by multiplying final examination score by two and adding points. Thus for person 1: $27 + 47 + 28 + 2(82) = 266$.

†Obtained by converting letter grades for each test to points ($A = 4$, $B = 3$, $C = 2$, $D = 1$, $F = 0$) weighting the points on the final by two, adding, and computing the weighted average. Thus for person 2: $3 + 4 + 4 + 2(4) = 19$; $19 \div 5 = 3.8$. Note that in computing a weighted average one divides the weighted average by the sum of the weights $(1 + 1 + 1 + 2)$.

‡Obtained by inspecting the relative ranges of scores on each test (15 for the first, 37 for the second, 13 for the third, and 61 for the fourth) and then roughly equating these by multiplying the first score by two and the third by three. Since the final examination score has a range already between one and one-half and two times the adjusted ranges of the other tests, it will have more weight and the final between two and one-half and three and one-half times as much weight as any of the others. These weighted raw scores are added and letter grades assigned to the weighted sums.

Suppose the score on the first test is multiplied by two and that on the third test by three. This brings their variabilities to about the same amount as that for the second test. Since it is intended that the final have twice as much weight, scores on it are not altered. Now when the weighted scores are combined (two times the first one plus the second one plus three times the third one plus the final) the scores recorded in column 14 are obtained. When these are then converted to letter grades, as in column 15, the letter grades can agree perfectly with those of column 13, which the student might compute for himself.

Again, the point being made is that the conversion to letter grades for the individual tests can effectively serve to equate the variabilities of measures later to be combined so that the students can know at any point where they stand. Moreover, the teacher does not have to attempt to explain corrections for unequal variabilities of the different tests that are due to artifacts of the scoring units.

In the foregoing illustrative data, the several sets of test scores were selected so as to be fairly highly correlated, so that the point being illustrated would not be obscured by the tendency of scores to regress toward the mean. Thus, for this illustration, all of the letter-grade distributions were very similar to the final one. In most cases, better results will be had if more students are assigned to the extremes than is anticipated for the final average based upon combining several letter grades.

THE CONCEPT OF CORRELATION

Most teachers will find very little time to compute correlation coefficients, and fortunately the need for them does not arise very often. Every teacher, however, needs some awareness of the *concept* of correlation and some may wish to compute an occasional coefficient.

Two variables that tend to vary together, with high scores in one associated with high scores in the other and low scores in one with low scores in the other, are *positively* correlated. If, on the other hand, high scores in one variable tend to go with low scores in the other and vice versa, the variables are *negatively* correlated. If the variables are unrelated, so that a high score on one is equally likely to be associated with a high score, a mediocre score, or a low score on the other, then the variables are *uncorrelated* or have about zero correlation. If, for a positive relationship, an increase in score for one variable is always associated with a corresponding increase in score for the other variable, a *perfect* positive relationship exists, denoted by a correlation coefficient (r) of 1.00. A perfect negative relationship is indicated by an r of -1.00. Lack of correlation is shown by coefficients that hover around .00.

The extent of relationship between two variables may be shown graphically by means of a *scatter plot* or *correlation chart*. This is a two-way table with the horizontal axis representing one variable *(X)* and the vertical axis representing the other variable *(Y)*. Low scores are at the left of the X-axis and at the bottom of the Y-axis. A tally mark is made for each individual in the cell at the intersection of the column corresponding to his X-score and the row corresponding to his Y-score. When the ranges of scores are greater than about twenty, the scores are commonly grouped into class intervals before the scatter plot is made. Inspection of the scatter plot will reveal whether there is a very high, moderately high, or relatively low correlation—either positive or negative—or whether it is about zero. To get the exact size of the coefficient, of course, requires some computation.

The following charts will illustrate in schematic form some different degrees of relationship.

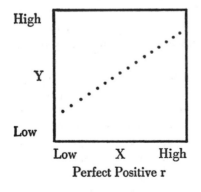

Perfect Positive r

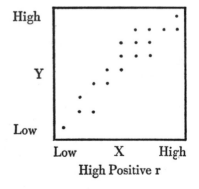

High Positive r

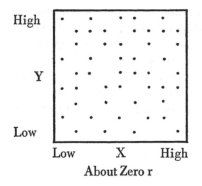

About Zero r

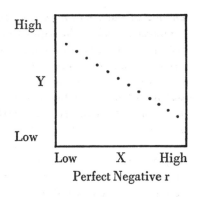

Perfect Negative r

The coefficient most commonly used, when the scores of both variables are distributed over several values, is the *Pearson product-moment coefficient*, symbolized by *r*. As previously indicated, it can range in value from −1.00 through zero to 1.00. Numerous other types of coefficients are applicable to special cases, as when one variable is multiple-categoried and one is dichotomous (takes just two values), when both variables are dichotomous, when special assumptions seem to be justified, or when the data are in the form of ranks. Descriptions of these various kinds of coefficients are available in statistics books. A chart for computing one, the *tetrachoric correlation coefficient*, will be presented later in the treatment of item analysis.

To compute a product-moment correlation coefficient for a small number of subjects, say less than one hundred, is no great chore. A method that is perhaps the easiest to explain is not the most efficient unless the number of cases is very small, say between twenty-five and forty. (If the number is less than this, usually computation of a correlation coefficient would not be warranted because of its sampling instability for small numbers of cases.) This method will be illustrated for the data on the first two tests on page 76, for just ten cases, even though *r*'s are not computed for such a small *n*. Test 1 will be referred to as X, Test 2 as Y. The symbol Σ, as before, means "the sum of." Thus ΣX is the sum of all ten X scores, ΣX² is the sum of the squares of all ten X scores, ΣY and ΣY² have corresponding meanings, and ΣXY means the sum of the ten XY products. The work is shown below. A person skilled with a calculating machine would not need to record the values in the X², Y², and XY columns but would cumulate the products in the machine to yield the desired totals.

Short-cut procedures using coded, grouped scores will effectively reduce the labor when the numerical scores and the number of cases are large. As indicated before, however, most teachers will not, in fact, be devoting time to computation of correlation coefficients. If they should find occasional need for one, their best course would be to consult a statistics book or to get some statistically inclined colleague to compute it for them.

Person	X	Y	X²	Y²	XY
1	27	47	729	2,209	1,269
2	23	55	529	3,025	1,265
3	19	45	361	2,025	855
4	19	42	361	1,764	798
5	17	33	289	1,089	561
6	15	28	225	784	420
7	14	27	196	729	378
8	14	18	196	324	252
9	12	18	144	324	216
10	25	23	625	529	575
Σ	185	336	3,655	12,802	6,589
	ΣX	ΣY	ΣX²	ΣY²	ΣXY

$$r_{XY} = \frac{n\Sigma XY - \Sigma X \Sigma Y}{\sqrt{[n\Sigma X^2 - (\Sigma X)^2][n\Sigma Y^2 - (\Sigma Y)^2]}}$$

$$= \frac{10(6,589) - (185)(336)}{\sqrt{[10(3,655) - (185)^2][10(12,802) - (336)^2]}}$$

$$= \frac{3,730}{\sqrt{(2,325)(15,124)}} = \frac{3,730}{5,929.865}$$

$$= .63$$

Chapter 9

Item Analysis

Item analysis refers to the application of statistical techniques to assess two characteristics of items, their difficulty and the extent to which they are correlated with other measures.

ITEM DIFFICULTY

The Concept of Difficulty

The most widely used interpretation of the difficulty of a test item is that *it is indicated by the proportion of the subjects who get the item right.* This proportion is really inversely related to the difficulty, because the larger the proportion getting an item right the easier the item. From long usage, however, the higher the difficulty index the easier the item is understood to be.

This notion of item difficulty is directly analogous to the idea that the average score on a test indicates how difficult the test is. Regard the score on the item as 1 if the response is correct and 0 if it is incorrect. If R equals the number of students who get the score of 1 and W the number who get the score of 0, then the average score for the total number of students $(R + W = n)$ will be

$$\frac{R \cdot 1 + W \cdot 0}{R + W} = \frac{R}{n}$$

Thus the proportion of the subjects who get the item right, the average score on the item, provides an index of item difficulty. The decimal point can be dropped if percentages are preferred to proportions. Sometimes D is used to indicate item difficulty, but p is perhaps more common. Thus:

$$p = 100 \frac{R}{n} \quad \text{or} \quad \frac{R}{n}$$

Recommended Procedures

For most achievement testing in the classroom, the average of the difficulty percentages of the items in a test should be about fifty. Opinions of test theorists still differ as to whether in general the items should all be of about 50 per cent difficulty or whether a fairly wide range of difficulty values with an average of fifty is preferable. This question is much more complicated than it seems, and this is not the place to present the technical details of the argument. For a single item, however, the maximum number of discriminations or elements of information that the item can provide is associated with the 50 per cent difficulty level. Thus if $n = 100$, it tells us that the fifty who get the item right are better on the function tested than the fifty who get it wrong. Thus 2,500 (50 x 50) elements of information are provided. Now if sixty (or forty) get it right, these sixty (or forty) are presumably better than the forty (or sixty) who get it wrong. We now have only 2,400 elements of information. For 70 or 30 per cent difficulty, we have 2,100; for 80 or 20 per cent difficulty, 1,600; for 90 or 10 per cent, 900; for 100 or 0 per cent, 0. Thus the 50 per cent difficulty level for a single item is optimal, other things being equal.

The situation becomes complicated by the intercorrelations of items when more than a single item is to be considered. All in all, however, the best course at the present time seems to be to aim in general at the 50 per cent level for most items. In the educational setting, however, at least a few items significantly easier and a few significantly more difficult than those at the 50 per cent level are normally included in an attempt to motivate the poorest student and to challenge the best.

As indicated earlier (pp. 37–38), for special purposes like selecting a small number of scholarship recipients or for sorting out only a small number of exceptionally poor learners, average difficulty should be much higher or much lower than the 50 per cent level.

The presumption throughout this discussion has been that all, or practically all, students have sufficient time to attempt every item. This should typically be the case for academic achievement tests except in the special circumstance when speed of performance on intrinsically easy items is being measured. In the latter case, indices of item difficulty would not be particularly useful in any case. If a severe time limit is placed on a power test, the effect on the difficulty measures for the later items in the test is in the direction of making them appear more difficult than they are when all students have an opportunity to consider them. Although one may compute the percentage correct for those students who attempt each item, this solution has drawbacks. Preferably, then, the best course is to have all students attempt all items.

ITEM DISCRIMINATING POWER

The Concept of Discriminating Power

Quite a different consideration is how well a test item is discriminating among the subjects. Ideally, for investigation of this property, an external criterion or an independent measure of that which is to be predicted should be available. In the selection of stenographers, for example, the relation of each item to an independent measure of success in stenographic positions might be explored. Various types of correlation coefficients might be used to express this relation, depending upon the particular form and characteristics of the data. In academic achievement testing, however, usually no independent measure is available as a criterion against which to assess the value of each item. In this situation, resort may be had to an internal criterion: score on the test of which the item is a part. Some measure of the relation of the individual item with the total test then is sought.

The assumptions are here implicit that the total test is measuring what it should be measuring and that the test can be improved by discarding items that are not positively correlated with the total score (or by selecting those that have a high positive correlation with the total score).

Another assumption in this approach is that the total test is measuring a unitary factor. If it is, in fact, measuring two or more quite different factors, then this type of item analysis may yield unfortunate results. If, for example, the teacher has combined into one test thirty items calling for quantitative ability and fifty items depending heavily on verbal ability, then blind application of item analysis using the total score on the eighty items as a criterion might well lead to the discard of the thirty quantitative items. The remedy would be to assess each of the quantitative items against the total score on the thirty quantitative items and each of the verbal items against the total score on the fifty verbal items. Thus if a total test contains clearly disparate sets of items, the total score can be broken down into separate components to serve as criteria for item analysis.

As many as fifty to sixty techniques for estimating the relation of a test item to a criterion score have been proposed. Many of these differ only slightly from others, and most can be regarded as approximations to a correlation coefficient for expressing the degree of relation between the item and the criterion. The more refined item analysis techniques are more likely to be applied to items in commercially distributed tests than to items in ordinary classroom tests. One of the reasons for this is that anticipated profits from a test to be sold will justify the accumulation of data on more subjects than typically are available for classroom tests. When a teacher's class contains fewer than perhaps one hundred students, expenditure of time on refined statistical indices for individual items is often not feasible. Upon occasion, however, the teacher may have a very large class or may collect data from several classes taking the same test so that some measure of the discriminating power of each item would be useful. A description of a method for serving this purpose that is computationally very simple will be provided, along with a less refined procedure that will require so little labor as to be profitable even for classes as small as twenty-five or thirty.

Recommended Procedures for Large n's

The first procedure, useful when the number of cases is, say, one hundred or above, calls first for splitting the group into two halves, upper and lower, on the criterion (often simply the total test score). Thus one group contains the upper half of the scores, the other the lower half. Next, the percentages of students in each of these two groups who pass a particular item are obtained. Using the computing chart on the following page, one locates the point along the vertical axis corresponding to the percentage in the upper group (p_u) and extends an imaginary line to the right, parallel to the horizontal axis. Then he locates the point along the horizontal axis corresponding to the percentage in the lower group (p_l) and extends an

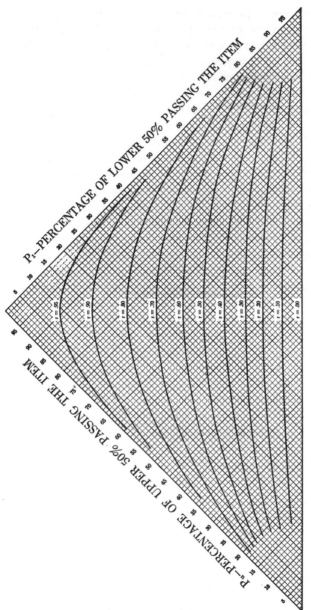

CHART FOR COMPUTING TETRACHORIC r
WITH THE CRITERION DICHOTOMIZED AT THE MEDIAN

Single copies of this chart will be furnished free of charge by the State of North Carolina Personnel Department, Raleigh, North Carolina. Additional copies can be purchased at the rate of $1.00 per dozen.

imaginary line downward parallel to the vertical axis. He then locates the intersection of these two lines and reads off the r value, interpolating as necessary. Thus for a p_u value of 58 and a p_l value of 30, r would be estimated as .45. Any necessary interpolation is done along the shortest distance (diagonal) between curves on the computing chart. If p_u is greater than p_l, the coefficient is positive. If p_l is greater than p_u, the coefficient is negative and is obtained by reversing the scales for p_l and p_u. As the percentages in the two groups passing the items approach 100 or 0, the coefficient is so greatly affected by chance that it cannot be estimated accurately. Its sign and general magnitude will be apparent, however.

The type of correlation coefficient yielded by the foregoing chart is known as a *tetrachoric* correlation coefficient. It assumes that both the item and the criterion variable are continuous and normally distributed. It uses, however, just two categories of information about both variables: pass or fail in the case of the item, and the upper or lower group in the case of the criterion.[1] Most authorities in the field of item analysis would not regard the tetrachoric coefficient, with its somewhat restrictive assumptions, as the best possible type of measure to use, but it is fairly frequently applied because of its computational ease.

Recommended Procedures for Small *n*'s

Even when the number of students for whom data are available is very small, the conscientious teacher will wish to have some notion about the validity of each item. When the percentage passing the item in the upper criterion group is higher than the corresponding percentage in the lower group, the item correlates positively with the criterion. When these two percentages are about equal, the item is serving no useful purpose, because its correlation with the criterion is approximately zero. When

---

[1] Tetrachoric correlation coefficients can be obtained when the criterion is split or dichotomized at a point other than the median, but the chart reproduced here is based upon a median split. The author first saw a similar chart developed by Marion W. Richardson around 1937 at The University of Chicago. Such a chart seems to have been published first in Charles I. Mosier and John V. McQuitty, "Methods of Item Validation and Abacs for Item-Test Correlation and Critical Ratio of Upper-Lower Difference," *Psychometrika*, V, No. 1, March 1940, pp. 57–65. Permission to use an adaptation of this chart has been obtained from the managing editor of the journal and from Dr. McQuitty. The chart presented here was developed under the author's direction at the North Carolina State Personnel Department.

significantly more students in the lower group than in the upper group select the right answer to an item (or when p_l exceeds p_u), the item actually has negative validity. Assuming that the criterion itself has validity, the item is not only useless but is actually serving to decrease the validity of the test.

Clearly, mere inspection of the relative sizes of the numbers in the upper and lower criterion groups will reveal whether the item-criterion correlation is positive, about zero, or negative. For some purposes, such inspection alone will suffice, saving the trouble of converting to percentages the numbers in each criterion group who pass the item, of reading the tetrachoric coefficients from a table, and of recording them.

Such an inspectional approach to the validity of individual test items can be coupled conveniently with an inspectional analysis of the way each alternative in a multiple-choice item is behaving. Although the number of students may be small, perhaps eighteen or twenty, the teacher who plans class discussion of a test, item by item, will find that an hour or two spent in analyzing the behavior of the supposedly wrong responses will be more than repaid by the resulting ease with which such a discussion can be conducted. Armed with data on each choice, the teacher can anticipate trouble spots. He will know most of the problems that will arise and have tentative solutions at hand.

The *validity* of an item is essentially the discriminating power of the right answer, as one category, versus all of the other alternatives lumped together as the other category. The resulting coefficient can be regarded as indicating the discriminating power or validity of the particular answer that is keyed as correct. By an analogous procedure, the validity of each answer regarded as poor or incorrect could also be investigated. Thus the correlation coefficient of each alternative, whether right or wrong, with the criterion may be obtained.

Ideally, each wrong answer should correlate negatively with the criterion in order for the item to have maximum validity. Extending the interpretation of positive and negative tetrachoric correlations as presented previously, any particular answer will have positive validity when the percentage choosing it among the upper group exceeds the percentage choosing it among the lower group (i. e., when p_u exceeds p_l). This state of affairs is undesirable if the particular answer is scored 0 rather than 1. Any alternative has the desired negative correlation when p_l exceeds p_u. The direction or sign of the relation for a particular alternative thus can be determined readily by inspection of the appropriate p_u and p_l values. The general order of magnitude of the relation for each answer can also be approximated by inspection.

As in the case of item difficulty indices, measures of item-criterion relationships are most readily interpretable for power tests, for which almost all subjects consider every item. For those items which a significant number of students do not reach or which a number of careless, poor students answer haphazardly, item validity indices are ambiguous. If anything, they are likely to be too high, but to an indeterminate extent. Again, however, most academic achievement tests should permit reasonably adequate time for almost all students to read the problems, so that typically no significant trouble should arise.

Illustrative Item Analysis Data

The procedures will become clear through an illustration. The first step again would be to split the group into upper and lower halves on the basis of criterion scores. Then a table for a particular item might appear as follows:

ITEM I

Choice	1	2*	3	4	5	
Upper 18	1	10	3	0	4	$r_t = .52$
Lower 18	0	4	6	1	7	$p = \dfrac{14}{36} = .39$
Total	1	14	9	1	11	

In this example, based upon only thirty-six cases, the keyed answer (indicated by an asterisk) has positive validity. From p_u (10/18) and p_l (4/18), the tetrachoric r can be read from the computing chart. Ordinarily a teacher would not bother to do this for a classroom test with only a small number of cases. The total percentage passing the item can be computed easily by dividing the sum of the numbers in both groups who chose the keyed answer by the total number of students. Having satisfied himself that the keyed answer has positive validity, the teacher then might inspect the relative frequencies in the two groups choosing each answer in turn. The upper number exceeds the lower number for the first answer, but no attention need be given to such a very small difference of frequen-cies. Although the differences between the groups are still quite small, the data for answers 3 and 5 show the desired negative validity. Again, the small difference for answer 4 warrants no attention. This item, then, is working as intended. One might try to revise answers 1 and 4 to make them more attractive to members of the lower criterion group if he planned to use the test again. Or he might decide that the item is working reason-ably well as it stands insofar as the data based upon a small n reveal a trend. In any case, he would clearly leave the scoring as originally planned for this particular group.

Now consider another diagram:

ITEM J

Choice	1	2	3	4*	5	
Upper 18	7	2	0	8	1	$r_t = .27$
Lower 18	2	6	3	5	2	$p = .36$
Total	9	8	3	13	3	

Inspection of the keyed answer reveals that it is working in the right direction, although the relation is not high. But see the data for answer 1. Clearly it would also have positive validity (actually about .55), even higher than that for the keyed answer. The other alternatives (2, 3, 5) are all operating in the intended direction.

At this point the teacher should inspect the item and carefully compare answers 1 and 4. Doubtless answer 4 will contain some obvious element of correctness. In any case, such data as these would not warrant count-ing it as incorrect. But inspection of answer 1 probably will reveal that, by some particular interpretation, it, too, has elements of correctness and should clearly be scored as correct. The solution here is to "double-key" the item, counting either answer 1 or answer 4 as correct, for this par-ticular group. The item should be revised before its next use, either by replacing one of these two answers or by making one of them more defi-nitely better or worse.

The validity of the item when it is double-keyed can be computed by combining the frequencies for alternatives 1 and 4 for the upper and lower groups in computing p_u and p_l. Thus p_u will be $(7 + 8)/18$ or .83 and p_l will be $(2 + 5)/18$ or .39. The corresponding r_t will be about .67. Students, incidentally, will accept this kind of evidence of why the scoring key should be adjusted much better than any amount of clamoring on the part of students who chose answer 1.

This diagram presents still another situation:

ITEM K

Choice	1	2*	3	4	5	
Upper 18	3	4	5	4	2	$r_t = -.22$
Lower 18	2	6	3	5	2	$p = .28$
Total	5	10	8	9	4	

Here the "best" answer, 2, has a low negative validity, while two "wrong" answers, 1 and 3, have low positive validities. The numbers in all of the cells are small, and the differences between the frequencies for the upper and lower groups very small indeed. This kind of pattern strongly suggests that, for this particular use of the item, all answers be counted as correct (which will simply have the effect of adding a constant to all scores) or all be counted as wrong.

Here is another situation:

ITEM L

Choice	1	2	3	4	5*	
Upper 18	1	2	10	3	3	$r_t = -.33$
Lower 18	0	4	3	5	6	$p = .25$
Total	1	6	13	8	9	

The keyed answer, 5, has negative validity, while an answer counted as wrong, 3, seems to have substantial positive validity. What can be wrong? Quite probably, a clerical error was made in constructing the scoring key, and answer 3 was intended all along to be the right answer. Such an error is thus detected readily and can be corrected at once. Or perhaps something essential was unintentionally omitted from the question or the keyed answer, so that, regardless of original design, the item constructor can now recognize that 3 is the better answer. Again, the key can readily be corrected.

Occasionally, the only solution will be to double-key the item in case an answer such as 5 still seems too nearly correct to be counted as wrong. In this instance, the double-keying would yield a tetrachoric that is positive but that is less than the correlation for answer 3 alone counted as correct. Double-keying would, of course, be an improvement over simply counting answer 5 as correct.

Such a diagram might arise in the case of some factual item for which answer 5 is clearly correct and answer 3 clearly wrong. This might come about if the fact were regarded by the better students as too trivial to be memorized or if they had some additional information that seemed to cast doubt on the correctness of answer 5. In such a case, the teacher would probably have to use the item for this particular group with answer 5 counted as correct and all others as incorrect. The item then would be discarded or revised before being used again.

Still another diagram will illustrate how readily a different type of item weakness can be revealed.

ITEM M

Choice	1*	2	3	4	5	
Upper 18	16	1	1	0	0	$r_t = .17$
Lower 18	15	0	1	2	0	$p = .86$
Total	31	1	2	2	0	

This item is simply too easy to yield much in the way of discrimination. Obviously, with only thirty-six cases, the small difference that is shown here between the numbers in the two groups choosing answer 1 clearly could be attributable to chance, as could the degree of positive relationship that is shown. A similar diagram could illustrate an item too difficult to be very discriminating.

Although in the foregoing diagrams total frequencies for each choice, r_t values, and p (difficulty) values have been shown for illustrative purposes, this bit of additional labor normally should be avoided for such a small group of subjects. The tetrachoric correlation coefficients, in particular, would be subject to considerable sampling instability. This means that the values one might find on his next sample of students would differ rather appreciably. Hence the very recording of the coefficients may tempt one to draw unwarranted conclusions.

Even with quite small numbers of students, however, a quick inspection of the frequencies in such a diagram for each item not only can serve as a check on the original scoring key but also can at once improve the validity of the test as scored with any corrections the analysis may indicate. Such an approach also provides useful data for indicating which items should be retained in their original versions, which discarded, and which revised before further use. Thus subsequent tests comprising items selected on the basis of analysis of this kind can be improved even more substantially.

Chapter 10

The Essay Test

DEFINITION

The essay form of test is the familiar one in which the test constructor supplies only the questions while the respondents compose the answers. Most frequently the number of questions to be answered in a given period of time is small, perhaps from one to three for one class period of forty or fifty minutes or from three to five or six for a double period. Usually as many variant answers are given as there are students taking the test, and the responses are expected to consist of anywhere from about half a page to four or five pages of prose.

The essential feature that differentiates the essay from the objective test resides in the form of the response. In one of the most objective types, the subject indicates his answer by checking the one of several alternatives that he believes to be the best. A clerk who knows nothing about the subject matter can compare his choices with predetermined answers. The probability that a second clerk will confirm the score obtained by the first one falls very close to unity. This characteristic of exceptionally high scorer reliability, of course, accounts for the term *objective test*. The response to an essay test question, on the other hand, is written by the subject in whatever manner he may deem appropriate. Thus he is free to choose the particular words with which to clothe his ideas and to organize them in his own way.

Note, however, that the student does not have complete freedom in preparing his response. It is expected to be relevant to the question asked. This restriction to less than complete freedom is by no means a drawback. In fact, through the painstaking incorporation of desirable restrictions in the framework of the question, the task of evaluating the answers can be saved from chaos.

PRESUMED ADVANTAGES OF THE ESSAY TEST

Testing Recall Rather Than Recognition

One frequently encounters the opinion that the serious weakness of objective tests is that they tap "mere recognition." The essay test is said to be preferable because it requires the subject to recall information.

Several early experiments bear on this question. When the same content was tested by multiple-choice tests and by the completion form in which the subject must recall and then supply missing material, scores were indeed somewhat higher for the recognition type. But the significant finding was that scores from the two forms were almost perfectly correlated. That scores on the multiple-choice form were higher is of no consequence, because the difficulty of such items can be controlled fairly easily. Hence if lower scores are desired for any reason—and usually there would be no reason—the difficulty can be increased.

Thus the correlation between highly reliable tests eliciting recall and those demanding only recognition is so high that for all practical purposes the scores are interchangeable. This finding would apply, of course, only when the generally lower scoring reliability of the less objective completion tests is carefully overcome. From the standpoint of scoring ease as well, the recognition form is preferable.

The claim that objective tests can appraise only recognition also conveys the implication that they must be restricted to material to which the subject has been exposed verbatim previously and thus that they can be used only to assess factual information. True, some objective tests as well as some essay tests do call for only factual information. This is not an inherent limitation of either form, however, but rather reflects a too common lack of ingenuity on the part of the test constructor.

Testing Higher-Level Mental Processes

As indicated above, objective tests frequently are disparaged by statements that they are limited by their very nature to the testing of factual information. Essay tests, it is claimed, in contrast lend themselves readily to appraisal of higher-level mental processes. These may be described variously as thinking, reasoning, conceptualization, abstract thinking, inference, induction, deduction, judgment, imagination, and so on. While such terms do not connote completely independent abilities, neither are they all synonymous. Statements about what abilities are tapped by essay tests are commonly based upon loose armchair analysis and only very rarely upon improved empirical approaches to the question of what abilities are tested, such as factor-analytic techniques.

Often, then, the examiner desires the essay question not only to elicit recall of learned material but also to require some organization of learned material, with the selection of that which is relevant and the discard of the remainder. Further, he may hope that the question itself will stimulate some novel integrations of the students' ideas or at the least call forth some new application of a familiar principle.

However rare the scientific isolation, identification, and differentiation of these higher-level mental abilities, probably essay tests can be developed that call many or all of them into operation in one guise or another. But so, we contend, can objective tests. It may even be argued that the identification of the abilities measured by the latter is much more likely, because their scores will not be confounded by the scoring unreliability that besets the typical evaluation of essay responses. Moreover, the tradition of statistical analysis is much more firmly entrenched for objective than for essay tests, so that the probability of ascertaining what is in fact being measured is substantially greater for objective tests.

Admittedly, however, objective tests are frequently confined largely to the testing of factual information. Be aware, however, that this is not an inherent characteristic of the form but a limitation of the item writer, who finds it easier to construct items on factual knowledge. Essay tests, too, despite the hope that they will reveal higher-level processes, often in fact call forth only well-practiced associations. Indeed, this may be true despite the fact that the question asks for reasons, other types of relationships, or examples. A response that meets all conditions imposed by the question may confine itself to the very reasons, relationships, or illustrations occurring in a reading assignment or in a classroom presentation. Recalling them and writing them down, even in new verbal combinations and sequences, does not entail reasoning so much as memory.

Like the objective form, however, the essay form can be used to test abilities that go beyond mere memory and that entail such processes as drawing correct inferences, educing principles or relationships, forming novel combinations of ideas, extending principles to new examples, and so on.

Lest the measurement of factual knowledge be dismissed as an unworthy goal of testing, one further point should be made. Reasoning, as well as other forms of higher-level mental behavior, does not transpire in a vacuum. One who lacks all knowledge of atomic physics does not reason in this field. Elements of knowledge, then, constitute essential ingredients of thought and reasoning—necessary but not, admittedly, sufficient. Often, then, the use of tests, either essay or objective, to appraise factual information is quite appropriate. Usually test objectives will go further, however, to encompass other goals as well.

Testing Originality or Creativity

Although *creativity* might have been included among the higher-level processes considered in the foregoing section, attempts to test this elusive quality present unique problems that warrant separate treatment. Creativity implies the production of something new, whether novel ideas or atypical compounds of old ones. Even though the idea or combination may have appeared before, it may be said to reveal creative ability if it is new to the individual who thought of it.

The ability to produce original ideas is to be distinguished from the ability to judge their relative merit. Some persons who evidence great creativity seem to be almost totally lacking in the ability to evaluate the worth of their ideas, while other more fortunate individuals are blessed both with a wealth of novel insights and the power to discriminate effectively among them. Thus creativity should be distinguished from judgment of the value or practicality of ideas.

Advocates of the essay test claim that it is impossible or at least very difficult to elicit creative behavior on the part of the subject in a completely objective test. Moreover, they note that if such behavior is not demanded by the test, it cannot be measured by the test. They are right.

The test, however, might consist of several rather definite or restricted problems to each of which the subject is to write a number of brief, original responses. Such a test would be of the nature of a short-answer or completion test with multiple responses permitted. The responses would have to be rated on some kind of scale of originality or the score might be the number of responses judged to meet some presumed standard of originality. To the extent that subjective judgment enters into the determination of the scores, however, the test is no longer highly objective. Clearly, it does not now consist of predetermined responses that the subject merely checks nor does it entail simply the counting of the number of responses made in a fixed period of time. The form of test under consideration may be regarded as a hybrid, partaking of some of the common features of objective tests (several items, numerous responses, brief responses) as well as some of the characteristics of the essay form (writing of answers in the subjects' own words, freedom of response within the limits set by the question). Attempts to assess creativity by such techniques as this, however, are still in their early stages and thus their wholesale application would be premature.

Now what of the more traditional essay form in relation to the testing of creativity? The essay form permits the subject to organize his ideas and present them in his own words if he so chooses, rather than parroting an answer that emanated from another source. In this feature of the essay test resides the possibility of evoking creative behavior, and therein lies the opportunity to foster it.

As others have noted, however, to encourage and occasionally to stimulate creative behavior without being able to measure it reliably is quite possible. For one thing, creative ability itself may be transient or unstable. It seems to fluctuate with conditions that as yet are understood too incompletely to permit their staging in a test setting. If the conditions under which creativity flowers cannot be established and controlled, the effect will be one of temporal instability of the trait measurement.

Allied to this effect is the fact that a creative response may not ensue readily at a predetermined time. Anecdotal accounts of great innovations lend support to this point of view that creative genius is not evinced upon immediate demand. The test setting doubtless is not the ideal environment in which to expect creative talent to manifest itself.

Another consideration has to do with content reliability. An individual who appears to be highly creative in dealing with one kind of problem may be quite devoid of ideas in approaching another situation. Thus the student who might demonstrate creativity in response to some essay questions might reveal very little in answering others. This result might be particularly likely if one question happened to coincide with a pronounced interest of his, while another was abhorrent to him. Hence whatever evidence of originality is shown may depend too much upon the particular content of the questions asked.

Still one more problem plagues the would-be tester of creativity. Someone, after all, must judge the originality of the student's responses—not their quality or their goodness in any sense, but rather their novelty from the point of view of the student who produced them. What at first sight appears to the judge to be a tired idea may after all be new to the student, and what he deems original may have come within the purview of the student before. Aside from the general problems of rating reliability that face the evaluator of essay responses, then, the special situation of trying to evaluate creativity seems to present even more formidable barriers.

PROBLEMS WITH THE ESSAY TEST

Lack of Scoring Economy

Unlike the objective test, the essay test cannot be assigned to a clerk for scoring. By its very nature, it requires the competent judgment of the expert in the relevant area of content.

Moreover, whereas an objective test may be scored in less than a minute, the careful evaluation of an essay may well consume from fifteen to thirty minutes, or even longer. When the average time per paper is multiplied by the number of students, the investment of time becomes indeed significant.

The wife of a popular professor who had not had a proper introduction to objective tests was wont to seek the sympathy of their friends because he was resigned to spending the entire period between semesters in marking examinations. Even then, his grade reports were not ready at the opening of a new term. With the prodding and assistance of a graduate student in a course in test construction, he learned how to develop adequate objective tests. Now his final examinations are all scored in less than half an hour per class by a test-scoring machine, and his final marks are assigned on the day of the final. As a result of his emancipation, he is an ardent advocate of time saving by means of objective tests. Nor does he feel that he is neglecting any of the significant goals of his course.

To suggest any feasible way in which the scoring time for essay test responses of a given length can be reduced significantly is manifestly impossible. The conscientious rater must read the responses if he is to evaluate them. True, through diligent practice he may increase his speed of reading handwriting that often is of indifferent quality at best. The time requirement will continue to be burdensome, however.

Another possibility, to be amplified later, is that the amount of writing required for the response to an essay question may be curtailed by thoughtful phrasing of the question itself. In other words, the restrictions incorporated in the question may serve to limit the length of the response and hence reduce the amount of reading.

Content Unreliability

Among the troublesome sources of test unreliability noted in chapter 3 was inadequate and unrepresentative sampling of the area of knowledge or behavior which is being measured. Thus for a particular examination, the teacher chooses a small proportion of the possible questions that he might pose. On the basis of the sample, he draws an inference as to the student's knowledge or ability in the universe of situations from which the sample was selected.

To the extent that the sample is small, it tends to be unrepresentative. A conclusion based on a small number of questions is very likely to be in error. A student who does well on one such sample will often do poorly on another similarly constituted. The correlation of ratings derived from two unrepresentative samples may approach zero, or at least be far short of a desirable reliability coefficient.

Thus a test containing only a few questions—perhaps three or four— may strike what students are prone to regard as chance gaps in their total behavioral repertoire. The students are loathe to recognize that such a test is equally likely to hit upon their chance strengths. Combined, these possibilities again mean simply that the scores on such a sample will not yield dependable inferences as to the students' over-all ability in the field concerned.

In the case of an objective test, which contains many times the number of questions that are in the typical essay test, the sampling is not necessarily good. With appropriate planning, however, the adequacy of the content sampling is much more readily controllable.

For the essay test, the best solution to the problem of poor content sampling seems to be to increase the number of questions and to make the questions quite precise so that the responses can be written in the time available. Thus an essay test of twelve to fifteen questions that can be answered fairly briefly can be expected to have markedly higher content reliability than a test of three or four questions.

Scorer Unreliability

The essay test is notoriously vulnerable to another source of test unreliability, the human error of the scorer.

A teacher might record his evaluations for a set of examinations on a separate sheet of paper and then put them aside until he has forgotten the specific answers given and the marks he assigned. Then he might repeat the scoring. Were he to do this, he might be astounded to note some of the discrepancies between the marks assigned to the same papers. He might go further and compute the correlation between the two sets of marks. Almost certainly it would not be a perfect positive correlation, and it might be as low as .40 or .50. Thus a rater often would not assign the identical mark twice to the same paper. To the extent that the rater tends to disagree with himself, so to speak, unreliability is present.

Now if two teachers were to mark the same set of papers independently, comparison of their ratings would reveal even more significant discrepancies. The correlation between the two sets of ratings of different teachers would be even less than the correlation between two sets of ratings made at different times by either of the teachers alone.

Unless many special precautions are taken, a rater of essay examinations is not likely to be perfectly consistent with himself and even less likely to agree with another rater. Although this is not the place to summarize the literature bearing upon the foregoing generalizations, much empirical evidence could be cited to substantiate them.

In contrast, the objective test has perfect or almost perfect rater reliability. As noted earlier, this is the feature from which the objective test derived its name.

The sources of rater unreliability are legion, but some are identifiable:
1. *The "Halo Effect."* The rater, reading through the responses to

several questions made by a single student, is subject to a type of error in judgment sometimes termed the "halo effect." This means that he may get an over-all impression of the quality of the paper that unduly influences his evaluations of answers to specific questions. If the first part of the paper impresses him favorably, for example, he may become more lenient in judging the last part. Or if the student blunders in answering a question dear to the heart of the teacher, the evaluation of the remainder of his paper may be adversely affected.

A partial remedy for the halo effect is for the teacher to read the responses of all students to a single question before going on to later questions. Also, if possible, the names of the students should not be revealed, but this procedure will not be effective for small classes.

2. *Influence of Extraneous Factors.* The judgment of the rater may be influenced by such factors as legibility or beauty of handwriting; quality of grammar, punctuation, diction, and spelling; or his impression as to the effectiveness of the organization of the material presented.

The remedy here is for the teacher to decide very definitely what separable features of the answers are to be evaluated and what ones are to be ignored if possible. Desirable though faultless grammar, choice diction, and impeccable spelling may be, the teacher may decide that the mark on a history examination should reflect knowledge of history rather than of English, which after all will be revealed by marks in English. If the teacher of history insists that the ability to write effectively is one of his objectives, then he should specify how many points, maximally, are to be allocated to quality of writing and just how different kinds and numbers of errors are to be penalized. Such a course is not recommended, however.

3. *Vagueness or Lack of Scoring Key.* Too often the teacher does not stop to define what constitutes responses of varying degrees of goodness. He may emerge from the reading of one answer with a general feeling that it is of pretty high quality and deserves perhaps eight points on a ten-point, ill-defined scale. Another answer, read several papers later, may contain all of the elements of the first and more. Memory is imperfect however, so it, too, may be assigned eight points or perhaps only six or seven. If the standards of evaluation are not clearly defined in the first place, they are very susceptible to fluctuation.

The solution to this problem is to prepare a tentative scoring key, deciding how many points are to be maximally assigned to each desired element of the answer. Then before any marks are assigned, several papers should be sampled to determine the adequacy of the key. It should be revised as indicated before final ratings are made.

4. *Restriction in Range of Scores.* Some teachers feel that a student who writes anything at all deserves some positive reward, or they forget that zero is just an arbitrary designation of a point on a scale. Believing that zero means complete absence of knowledge, they are reluctant to admit that any student whom they have tried to teach knows nothing. Hence they are trapped into assigning perhaps four or five to the worst answers they find. If the same teachers believe that ten represents perfection and that no student can be perfect, they may end with a scale restricted to the range of four or five to eight or nine instead of using the ostensible zero to ten scale. Restriction in the number of different scores assigned results in coarser discrimination than is necessary and thus contributes to unreliability.

The advance preparation of a scoring key, specifying the number of points to be assigned to each component or aspect of the answer, should also alleviate this problem of an undesirably narrow range of scores.

5. *Residual Subjectivity.* Even when all of the remedial measures suggested above are applied, scores on essay tests still often fall short of perfect scoring reliability. Such a situation may not be tolerable, especially when a very important outcome, such as a scholarship, hinges upon the results of the examination. One final step may then be taken. The evaluations of two or more equally competent raters may be pooled. Preferably these ratings should be made independently. After a few papers have been rated, however, the marks should be compared. If large discrepancies appear, the raters may be interpreting the scoring key differently. Discussion of the sources of the differences will usually result in a more uniform interpretation of the key and hence more consistent scores.

IMPROVING THE ESSAY TEST

Means for improving the essay test stem quite directly from consideration of the special problems that they present. For this reason, several remedial suggestions have been presented earlier as each disadvantage was being discussed. These may now be summarized under two general headings, measures dealing with the preparation of the questions and those related to marking practices.

Rules for Developing Essay Test Questions

1. *The teacher must plan to devote sufficient time to constructing the questions.*

Unfortunately, essay questions are often carelessly dreamed up as the teacher goes to class and are not even composed until the teacher reaches the blackboard. The resulting tests are very likely to reveal a number of defects—poor sampling of content, ambiguity, generality, and certain lack of a predesigned scoring key. As will be noted later, the construction time should be long enough to permit not only careful phrasing of the questions but also development of a detailed scoring key. Often the teacher's attempt to write down a key will reveal basic weaknesses in the questions. If this step is ensured before the test is given, the questions can be revised to overcome their faults at the appropriate time.

Perhaps a good general rule is that an essay test should take at least as much time to construct as the students will require to answer it.

2. *The questions should precisely define the direction and scope of the answers desired.*

Each essay question should be unambiguously interpretable by the respondents. Though some may not know the answer, all should have a clear idea as to what question is being posed. The question itself may well incorporate instructions as to the intended coverage of the answers and the amount of detail desired. If the question is unclear, then the students are not running the same race. If some respond to the question the teacher intended to ask while others provide their own different but legitimate interpretation of it, then the responses cannot be rated on the same scale. If the rating scales for different students are not the same, the marks assigned cannot provide information as to the relative competence of the students.

Probably the worst offender among essay questions is the typical exhortation to discuss something. Suppose, for example, that one wished to write an essay question to sample understanding of the content of this chapter. The first attempt of the novice might yield the following question:

Discuss the essay test.

The hapless student would scarcely know where to begin, and he would surely not know where to end. He would probably resort to writing in a more or less aimless fashion until he judged his time allotment had been consumed.

An improved question might read:

> Contrast the essay test form with the objective test form as to (1) validity, (2) reliability, and (3) economy.

Or it might be detailed as follows:

> Cite the major advantages and disadvantages of the essay test, giving specific suggestions for improving the typical essay test.

Or:

> Contrast essay and objective tests, indicating the major advantages and disadvantages of each from the points of view of measurement theory and practice.

With any one of the last three questions, as compared with the first, the teacher will find that his task of developing a scoring key is markedly facilitated. This is true because he has provided himself, in the very framework of the question, with a much more definite idea of the type of response he is seeking to elicit.

3. *A large number of questions each of which demands a short answer is often preferable to a small number of questions calling for long answers.*

An essay test including a large number of questions, say ten to fifteen, in contrast to a test of one to four questions, has the advantage of more adequate sampling of the universe of content concerned. Also, questions designed for briefer answers are usually more precise. Sometimes it is practical to convey to the student the desired length of answer or amount of detail by duplicating the questions on sheets that contain appropriate space for answering each.

Some narrower questions than those presented above dealing with the content of this chapter are as follows:

> Contrast essay and objective tests as to their adequacy in appraising attainment of educational goals.
> How can the content reliability of essay tests be improved?
> Briefly give several suggestions for improving the scoring reliability of essay tests.
> Why is the advance preparation of a scoring key for essay tests often advocated?
> How can the "halo effect" in the rating of essay test papers be reduced?

Any one of these questions can be answered in a few minutes.

4. *The time available for responding to the question should be carefully considered in relation to the amount of writing required for adequate responses.*

One of the major problems in the use of essay tests is that frequently no one could plan and write a completely satisfactory answer to all of the questions in the time allowed. Even when some students who write rapidly have been able to answer all of the questions, the ones who write more slowly are often unable to complete the test. If they are simply given no credit for questions that they really did not have time to attempt, the resulting scores represent an ambiguous hodgepodge, with degree of understanding of subject matter confounded with speed of writing. Probably the basic reason why essay tests have tended to be too long is that the teacher is unconsciously trying to compensate for what he vaguely realizes is inadequate coverage of the content to be sampled.

Although there is doubtless a point at which slow writing is causally related to slow thinking rather than to inferior motor habits, the teacher should ensure that the time allowance for the essay test is sufficient. If he is convinced that the sampling of content will be inadequate with a reduction in the number of questions, he can perhaps apply the idea of using more questions requiring briefer answers. Or he may decide that an objective test would be worthwhile.

5. *The same examination should be administered to all the students whose relative degrees of achievement in a particular area are to be compared.*

The purpose of an educational achievement test is usually to evaluate the degree to which each student has attained a composite of educational goals. The various performances of the students are to be compared on a scale representing different degrees of achievement of the goals, as evidenced by test responses. Clearly the scale points denoting different qualities of performance are much more likely to be comparable if all students have faced the same set of test situations. This means that the practice of providing optional essay items, essentially permitting each student to plan his own examination, is generally indefensible. If several choices between alternative questions are available, the result may be that no two students have taken the same examination.

The earlier discussion of this matter of optional items noted that the practice is much more common for essay than for objective tests, because the essay tester finds himself uncomfortable in contemplating the poor content sampling of the ordinary essay test. (See p. 41.) He might better resort to other solutions of this problem than to give different tests to different students.

The use of optional questions is possibly defensible for examinations for graduate degrees when the students have not been exposed to identical curricula, as previously noted (pp. 41–42). For students enrolled in a particular course of study, however, no sound argument for the use of optional questions can be adduced.

Rules for Evaluating Essay Test Papers

1. *Preferably at the time the test is constructed, the teacher should prepare a tentative scoring key.*

As noted earlier, the development of a scoring key will often reveal weaknesses in the structure of a question that can be corrected prior to its use. The scoring key shows, first, how many points are to be allotted maximally to each question. It then indicates the particular elements in a fully acceptable answer, with the number of points allowable for each.

At the time the key is under preparation, the teacher should decide what is to be done about errors in grammar, punctuation, spelling, and the like; about quality of handwriting; and about logical organization of subject matter. Most authorities would probably recommend that errors in grammar, punctuation, and spelling be noted for all essay papers but not penalized except for English courses. They would suggest that every effort be made not to allow handwriting to influence scores. They might differ, however, in recommendations regarding the organization of subject matter, some feeling that good organization reflects a desirable educational goal in any content area and thus that it should be rewarded. In any event, they would all agree that the teacher should make a definite decision on whether or not to allow points for the logical organization of material, rather than letting some general impression of the quality of a paper's organization vaguely prod the score upwards or downwards.

2. *The tentative key should be applied to an assortment of answers as a preliminary check on its adequacy.*

The teacher may find in trying out the key that he has overlooked some important element in an answer that shows up in one or more responses. He can then incorporate this element into his key. He may see that his original key results in a very narrow range of scores. Sometimes he can alter the key to yield a greater degree of discrimination. Upon occasion, the trouble may be with the intrinsic difficulty of a question that is too easy or too hard to be discriminating. In this case, although he cannot change the immediate situation, he can profit from the experience.

3. *In order to reduce "halo effect," one question should be graded seriatim for all respondents rather than all questions seriatim for one respondent.*

The undesirable effect that an over-all impression (or the impression from the first few questions) may have upon judgments of answers to different questions is known as the "halo effect." It can be at least partially overcome by grading responses to each question for all students before proceeding to the next question.

4. *If a large number of papers must be graded, the teacher should periodically recheck papers graded earlier to ensure that standards have not shifted appreciably.*

Particularly when the number of papers to be graded is so large as to require several grading periods, separated in time, the teacher's standards may shift in one direction or the other. An occasional recheck of a few papers marked earlier will help to overcome any such tendency towards non-comparable standards. The teacher should also be aware that a mediocre response may seem excellent after a sequence of several very poor answers and inferior after several very good ones.

5. *When resources permit and an essay test has unusually important consequences, the pooled ratings of equally competent judges should be obtained because they are more reliable than the ratings of a single judge.*

Usually a single teacher has the full responsibility for assigning marks in a course of instruction. In view of the empirically demonstrated low rater reliability of many essay examinations, however, a special effort should be made to obtain two or more raters for highly important essay examinations. Such might be the case when a scholarship is at stake, or when an athletic coach is on tenterhooks at the teacher's doorstep, waiting to learn whether a prospective Olympic Games competitor is to get a D minus or an F—an actual case, by the way, in which the professor in charge of the course concurred in the D minus assigned by the instructor.

Appendix A

ILLUSTRATION OF AN OBJECTIVE APPROACH
TO MEASURING SCIENTIFIC THINKING[1]

This series of objective test items was a part of a test administered to students entering the Chicago City Junior College who wished to enroll in the second semester of a physical science survey course.

... A scientist, when confronted with a problem, formulates hypotheses which represent tentative solutions to the problem. He then collects data which may support or disprove his hypotheses. Finally, on the basis of the data and the hypotheses thus tested, he derives a conclusion which constitutes his answer to the problem.

The following exercises represent an effort to test your ability to do some scientific thinking. You are to test certain true or false hypotheses, and to evaluate certain general conclusions. Assume that each item of data below each hypothesis is a true statement and *may* directly or indirectly help to prove an hypothesis true or false.

If the application of the item of data requires only one step to prove he truth or falsity of an hypothesis, then the item is *direct* help. For example, the temperatures of water boiling on a given mountain and at sᶠa level would represent *direct* evidence of the falsity of the hypothesis "water boils at a higher temperature on a mountain than at sea level."

If the application of the item of data requires more than one step to prove the truth or falsity of an hypothesis, then the item is an *in-*

---

[1]Reprinted by permission from Max D. Engelhart and Hugh B. Lewis, "An Attempt to Measure Scientific Thinking," *Educational and Psychological Measurement*, I (1941), pp. 289–94.

direct help. For example, the item "water in a container that can be evacuated will boil at room temperature" *indirectly* helps to prove the falsity of the hypothesis "water boils at a higher temperature on a mountain than at sea level."

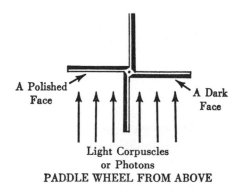

Light Corpuscles
or Photons
PADDLE WHEEL FROM ABOVE

A number of years ago Sir William Crookes perfected an instrument which always intrigues people, whether laymen or scientists. This is the radiometer, a device consisting essentially of a paddle wheel which is free to rotate in a horizontal plane within a partially evacuated glass bulb. One side of each paddle is brightly polished, while the other side is coated with lampblack. As soon as the device is placed in the sunlight, the little paddle wheel starts to spin rapidly. It continues to spin until the device is again placed in the dark. PROBLEM: *How does sunlight cause the paddle wheel to rotate?*

Below are given a series of hypotheses, each of which is followed by numbered items which represent data. After each item number on the answer sheet blacken space

A if the item directly helps to prove the hypothesis true.

B if the item indirectly helps to prove the hypothesis true.

C if the item directly helps to prove the hypothesis false.

D if the item indirectly helps to prove the hypothesis false.

E if the item neither directly nor indirectly helps to prove the hypothesis true or false.

HYPOTHESIS I: *In a partial vacuum the paddle wheel rotates because of the impact of photons of light.*

1. Scientists now believe that light has both corpuscular and wave characteristics.
2. In a very high vacuum the bright faces of the paddle wheel turn slowly away from the light, while the black faces turn toward the light.
3. Light travels at the rate of 186,000 miles per second.
4. In a partial vacuum the black faces of the paddle wheel turn away from the light, while the bright faces turn toward the light.
5. Light travels at a slower speed in glass than in air or in a vacuum.
6. After *this* item number on the answer sheet blacken space A if Hypothesis I is true, or space B if it is false.

HYPOTHESIS II: *A paddle wheel on which all of the faces are bright or all are black will not rotate.*

7. The black faces of paddles absorb energy from light to a greater extent than the bright faces of paddles.
8. Rotation is due to force of impact. If all paddles are the same on both sides, either all bright or all black, the turning forces would cancel.
9. More photons rebound from bright faces than from dark faces.
10. In a partial vacuum, air molecules are constantly hitting the paddles.
11. Photons are hitting the sides of the paddles which face the light.
12. After *this* item number on the answer sheet blacken space A if Hypothesis II is true, or space B if it is false.

HYPOTHESIS III: *Rotation in a partial vacuum of the paddle wheel is due to the greater force of rebound of air molecules from the black faces than from the bright ones.*

13. The bright faces remain cooler than the dark faces, since they reflect more light.
14. In a partial vacuum and in the dark the paddle wheel will rotate when exposed to invisible infrared rays from a warm flatiron.
15. The black faces of the paddles become warmer than the bright faces, since they absorb more light.
16. Air molecules adjacent to the warmer black faces rebound from these faces with greater energy than from the cooler bright faces.
17. In a very high vacuum and in the dark the paddle wheel will rotate slowly if invisible rays from a cathode tube are directed toward it.
18. After *this* item number on the answer sheet blacken space A if Hypothesis III is true, or space B if it is false.

Below are five conclusions. After each corresponding number on the answer sheet blacken space

A If in your judgment the conclusion is the best answer to the problem.

B If in your judgment the conclusion is neither the best answer nor the least satisfactory answer to the problem. (Three conclusions should receive this mark.)

C if in your judgment the conclusion is the least satisfactory answer to the problem.

19. The paddle wheel of the radiometer rotates, because air molecules move with greater energy when heated by energy from sunlight or from infrared rays from a flatiron.

20. Air molecules rebound with greater force from the bright faces, which reflect more light energy. Photons rebound from dark faces to a greater extent than from bright faces. The turning forces thus created cause black faces to rotate toward the light in a partial vacuum and away from the light in a very high vacuum.

21. The paddle wheel of the radiometer rotates, because photons of light strike air molecules with greater energy when adjacent to the dark faces than when adjacent to the bright faces.

22. The fact that a radiometer will operate in either a partial or a very high vacuum demonstrates that it is not essential that air molecules be present in order to cause rotation.

23. Air molecules rebound with greater force from the black faces, which absorb more light energy than the bright faces. Photons rebound from bright faces to a greater extent than from dark faces. The turning forces thus created cause black faces to rotate away from the light in a partial vacuum and toward the light in a very high vacuum.

Appendix B

ILLUSTRATIVE MULTIPLE-CHOICE ITEMS[1]

For each item, indicate the number of the best answer.

_____In a region in which are found caves, sinkholes, and natural bridges, one would also be most likely to find
  (1) dikes.   (4) stalactites and stalagmites
  (2) petrified tree trunks.   (5) talus slopes.
  (3) laccoliths and batholiths.

_____The chief factor in the production of black or humus soils is the action of
  (1) running water.   (4) cultivation and grazing.
  (2) differential erosion.   (5) ground water.
  (3) bacteria on organic material.

_____A geologist finds a certain species of trilobite in a limestone quarry near Chicago. He finds other examples of the same fossil in limestone strata near Niagara Falls and concludes that both limestone formations are of about the same age. This geologist has used the law of
  (1) uniformitarianism.
  (2) superposition.   (4) intrusion.
  (3) unconformity.   (5) organic correlation.

[1]Adapted by permission from examination materials developed under the direction of Dr. Max D. Engelhart, Chicago City Junior College.

_____The entrenched meanders and rejuvenated streams of the present Appalachian Mountains are evidence of
(1) the formation of a new geosyncline.
(2) the occurrence of crustal shortening resulting in re-elevation.
(3) glacial action.
(4) slipping and faulting.
(5) the presence of alternate layers of hard and soft rocks.

_____Which of the following constitutes the best definition of a public?
(1) A group of people who have the same political convictions and who may be expected to vote alike on a given issue.
(2) A group of people who are interested in the same issues and who are interested in working out common solutions to these issues.
(3) A group of people who receive their information from the same sources—newspapers, radio programs, and magazines.
(4) A group of people who have the same release of inhibitions, loss of responsibility, and sense of anonymity.

_____In a certain area in a metropolitan city the delinquency rate has remained high for forty years, although during that time German, Scandinavian, Irish, Italian, and Negro populations have succeeded one another in this area. This probably means that
(1) the tendencies toward delinquency have not changed in forty years.
(2) in this area the accepted definitions of delinquent behavior have not changed in forty years.
(3) during these forty years this area has continued to be located in the transition area of the city.
(4) each delinquent, as he grows up, has many associates, whom he teaches delinquent habits.

_____In the state of Maine, a very successful project in dealing with the problem of homeless old men has been established. The cost of this project has been greatly reduced as a result of the work done by the old men themselves in building, painting, repairing, and in raising vegetables and chickens. It is probable that the success of the project can best be credited to the
(1) economical way the project is run.
(2) restoring of a sense of status to the men.

(3) healthful conditions of a rural environment.

(4) elimination of alcoholism and drug addiction.

_____Which of the following factors has the greatest effect on the velocity of sound in air?

(1) The temperature of the air.

(2) Changes in atmospheric pressure near the earth's surface.

(3) The loudness of the sound.

(4) The energy associated with the sound wave.

(5) The pitch or frequency of the sound.

_____The term used in connection with sound which corresponds to color with reference to light is

(1) pitch.   (4) intensity.

(2) timbre.   (5) harmony.

(3) tone.

_____A beam of light passes through a small hole in a screen, and illuminates a circular area on a second screen. Some of the light passes through two holes within the illuminated area on the second screen to form two illuminated but overlapping circular areas on a third screen. Where the two areas overlap alternate bright and dark lines appear. This experiment supports the theory that light

(1) can be reflected.   (4) does not travel through

(2) is a form of wave motion.   a vacuum.

(3) consists of photons.   (5) exhibits the Doppler
                                            effect.

_____Which of the following facts supports a modern corpuscular, or particle, theory of light rather than the wave theory?

(1) Light travels three-fourths as fast in water as in air.

(2) Light is diffracted on passing through a small opening.

(3) The velocity of travel of electromagnetic waves is the same as the velocity of light.

(4) Light immediately causes ejection of electrons in a photoelectric tube.

(5) Light exhibits interference and reinforcement effects.

_____Which of the following constitutes direct observational evidence that the orbit of the earth is an ellipse rather than a circle?

(1) Measurement of the orbits of the other planets has shown them to be elliptical rather than circular.

(2) Variation in the sun's apparent size.

(3) Observation of the changing plane of swing of a Foucault pendulum.

(4) Variation in length of the mean solar day.

(5) Observation of the sun's apparent path among the stars.

_____A solar day would exactly equal a sidereal day if the

(1) orbit of the earth were a circle.

(2) earth would rotate a little more rapidly.

(3) earth would rotate a little less rapidly.

(4) earth did not revolve, but continued to rotate.

(5) solar day did not vary in length during a year.

_____The ecliptic and the celestial equator would be the same if the

(1) axis of the earth were at 90° to the plane of the earth's orbit.

(2) orbit of the earth were not an ellipse.

(3) equator of the earth were not in the same plane as the celestial equator.

(4) North Pole did not point toward Polaris.

(5) orbit of the earth were not in the plane of the ecliptic.

_____All through history the production of a satisfactory calendar has been a troublesome problem largely because

(1) months vary in their number of days.

(2) the time between two arrivals of the sun at the vernal equinox is 365.2422 mean solar days.

(3) only in recent times has the problem been well understood.

(4) modern clocks and telescopes were needed to attack the problem.

(5) it was necessary to know that the earth revolves about the sun.

_____Which of the following pairs of things can be measured by essentially the same instrument?

(1) Altitude and relative humidity.

(2) Temperature and atmospheric pressure.

(3) Atmospheric pressure and altitude.

(4) Wind velocity and relative humidity.

(5) Wind velocity and atmospheric pressure.

_____The N.E. trade winds blow toward the southwest while the S.E. trade winds blow northwest. This is true

(1) because the earth rotates toward the west.

(2) only because the earth rotates toward the east.

(3) because the anti-trade winds are deflected eastward.

(4) because the earth rotates and it is hotter at the equator than elsewhere.

(5) only because the "horse latitudes" are regions of low pressure while there is a region of high pressure along the equator.

———Any actual remains, molds, casts, or tracks left by a plant or animal of past geologic times is called

(1) a geological object.   (4) a fossil.

(2) an archeological object.   (5) a petrification.

(3) a proof of evolution.

———Direct evidence of evolutionary change in the life of the past is offered by

(1) domestication.   (4) the fossil record.

(2) experimental breeding.   (5) natural selection.

(3) isolation.

Appendix C

ILLUSTRATIONS OF VARIOUS FORMS OF MULTIPLE-CHOICE ITEMS IN SEVERAL FIELDS[1]

For each item, write

    1 if the item is true of proteins.

    2 if the item is true of fats.

    3 if the item is true of carbohydrates.

    4 if the item is true of vitamins.

    5 if the item is true of minerals.

_____Intake is controlled in the treatment of diabetes.

_____Are a necessary constituent of bones.

_____Their presence is independent of photosynthesis and of the products of photosynthesis.

_____The bile salts function in their digestion.

_____Are largely carried to the heart without first passing through the liver.

    Etc.

For each item, write

    1 if the item at the *left* of the page is greater than the item at the right.

    2 if the item at the *right* of the page is greater than the item at the left.

[1]Adapted by permission from examination materials developed under the direction of Dr. Max D. Engelhart, Chicago City Junior College.

3 if the two items are of essentially the same magnitude.

_____Extent to which antitrust legislation has broken up monopolies as a result of court decisions.

Extent to which the threat of more drastic legislation has tended to prevent the increase of monopoly power.

_____Extent to which the interpretation of the word "restraint" in the Sherman Act as "unreasonable restraint" has helped to curb monopoly power.

Extent to which the interpretation of the word "restraint" in the Sherman Act as "unreasonable restraint" has helped to promote monopoly power.

_____Extent to which the existence of monopoly is justified in the case of ordinary corporations.

Extent to which the existence of monopoly is justified in the case of public utilities.

Etc.

For each item, write

1 if the item is true of the Monroe Doctrine.

2 if the item is true of the Open Door Policy.

3 if the item is true of both the Monroe Doctrine and the Open Door Policy.

4 if the item is true of neither the Monroe Doctrine nor the Open Door Policy.

_____By adopting this policy the United States sought to safeguard important interests of the American people.

_____According to this policy the interests of the United States take precedence over those of any European country.

_____Violation of this policy occasioned the enunciation of the "Stimson Doctrine."

_____Our traditional policy of freedom of the seas is basic to this policy.

Etc.

For each item, write

1 if the statement is *most* characteristic of mercantilism.

2 if the statement is *most* characteristic of liberalism.

3 if the statement is *most* characteristic of socialism.

4 if the statement is *most* characteristic of communism.

5 if the statement is *most* characteristic of Fascism or Nazism.

_____Advocates, in addition to the collective ownership of capital goods, the collective ownership of some or all forms of consumers' goods.

_____Collective ownership of the means of production should evolve from the present competitive system.

_____Exports should be encouraged and imports hampered.

Etc.

Each of the following exercises begins with mention of two things which are in some way related. For each item, write the number which designates the statement suggesting the *most significant relationship* between the two things. (A statement may be correct, but not an expression of the most significant *relationship*.)

_____Invisible government — Spoils system:

(1) The control of a political organization by one or a few men.

(2) The use of the merit system in making political appointments.

(3) The use of the "social lobby" to gain control of government.

(4) The machine's control of patronage to influence the operation of government.

_____Pressure groups — Public opinion:

(1) The use of the "social lobby" by special interest groups to influence government.

(2) The use of lobbyists to influence legislation.

(3) The use of various techniques to arouse widespread support on specific issues.

(4) The resolution of issues through the reconciliation of divergent views.

_____Democratic process — Social values:

(1) The introduction of the direct primary is part of the democratic process.

(2) The social values of our democracy are our ideals.

(3) The social values set the goals which we attempt to reach through the democratic process.

(4) The existence of invisible government hinders the operation of the democratic process.

_____Pressure groups — Legislators:

(1) A special interest group that works for its own interests characterizes a pressure group.

(2) The use of lobbyists to influence legislation is a very important technique used by pressure groups.

(3) The legislators are charged with making the laws of the nation.

(4) The existence of pressure groups demonstrates a basic weakness of our democratic system.

Etc.

For each item, write the number which designates the word or phrase in the list below that would correctly complete the statement.

1 Zero, or continuously zero.

2 Continuously a constant amount not zero.

3 Zero, then a constant amount greater than zero, then zero again.

4 Continuously variable in amount.

(Assume no air resistance and no friction.)

_____If a car is moving along a straight road at constant speed, the force is _____.

_____A uniformly changing speed along a straight line is produced by a force which is _____.

_____A ball is thrown upward into the air with an initial speed of 64 ft./sec. The speed of the ball while in the air is _____.

_____A body is projected horizontally with an initial speed of 64 ft./sec. from a point 256 ft. above the ground. Its speed in the vertically downward direction is _____.

Etc.

Diction and idiom. For each of the following sentences, write the appropriate number to show that the sentence contains

1 a slang or colloquial expression.

2 a word that does not mean what the author intended.

3 a trite or hackneyed expression.

4 a redundant expression (using unnecessary words).

5 an idiom formed with the wrong preposition.

_____He felt kind of embarrassed, but could think of nothing to say.

_____With a sigh of relief, she revealed her deep, dark secret.

_____People over forty should not exercise themselves too strenuously.

_____There were a dozen ways to spend the unexpected holiday, and we couldn't decide between them.

_____This award encouraged him on to keep up his art studies.

Etc.

===

In the following sentences, write the appropriate letter to designate the correct form of the pronoun.

_____John's brother is much taller than (A. he; B. his; C. him).

_____We had not heard of (A. he; B. his; C. him) leaving school last semester.

_____Was it they (A. who; B. whose; C. whom) we met at the Art Institute?

_____(A. Who; B. Whose; C. Whom) do you suppose will win the scholarship?

Etc.

===

Use of verbs. In each of the following pairs of sentences, one sentence contains a faulty verb, mistaken either in tense or form. For each pair, mark the correct or acceptable sentence.

_____A. As a result of following a few simple rules of safety, I had no accidents during these last ten years.

B. The subject matter of many children's programs actually appeals mainly to adults.

_____A. He loved to haggle, and if he was directly asked the price of an article he would begin to haw and hum.

B. If I was capable of such spiteful feelings, I'd certainly try to hide them.

_____A. His jokes are of a type that seem to appeal to everybody.

B. I wish I had been able to go with you.

_____A. After we had swam to the raft, we sunned ourselves thoroughly.

B. That cat just sits wherever you set him.

Etc.

Grammar. Certain portions of the paragraph below are numbered and underlined. Mark the correct identification or description of the underlined element.

Science-fiction is that branch of
$\overline{209}$

literature that is concerned with the
$\overline{210}$

impact of scientific advance upon hu-
$\overline{210}$

man beings. The most important part
$\overline{210}$

of that definition is that science-fiction
$\overline{211}$

deals first and foremost with human
$\overline{211}$

beings. This point should not be over-
$\overline{211}$ $\overline{212}$

looked. It is possible to write good
$\overline{212}$ $\overline{213}$ $\overline{214}$

science-fiction about a robot
$\overline{215}$

209. A. Subject
B. Subjective complement (predicate nominative)
C. Object

210. A. Main or independent clause
B. Restrictive clause
C. Nonrestrictive clause

211. A. Noun clause
B. Adjective clause
C. Adverb clause

212. A. Complement of a verb
B. Phrase modifier
C. Predicate

213. A. Adjective
B. Adverb
C. Noun

214. A. Infinitive
B. Gerund
C. Participle

215. A. Subordinate clause
B. Prepositional phrase
C. An appositive

Punctuation and mechanics. The following passages are excerpts from a magazine book-review column, altered for the purposes of this test. Below the line of text are numbers corresponding to the item numbers.

From the column on the right, indicate the best version in each case. *Note that in some instances no change is required.*

A book which I enjoyed, Animal
    1   2

Tools by George F. Mason, Morrow,
  2   3

$2.00, drew an approving whistle
      3

from Ronnie my apprentice, also. "Its
         4   5

the nuts, he said. "Look, it shows the
    6

way frogs goggles start from the lower
    7

part of their eyes and it shows how the
        8

light comes from a fireflys stomach.
                   9   10

1. A. A book which
   B. A book, which

2. A. *Animal Tools*
   B. "Animal Tools"

3. A. Mason, (Morrow,
      $2.00) drew
   B. Mason (Morrow,
      $2.00), drew

4. A. Ronnie my apprentice,
      also
   B. Ronnie, my apprentice,
      also

5. A. "Its
   B. "It's

6. A. the nuts," he
   B. the nuts", he

7. A. frogs'
   B. frog's

8. A. eyes and
   B. eyes, and

9. A. fireflies'
   B. firefly's

10. A. stomach."
    B. stomach".

For each item, write a number to indicate that the statement applies to
  1. *Medea.*
  2. *Hedda Gabler.*
  3. both plays.
  4. neither play.

———On the first presentation of the play the audience came to the theatre already familiar with the general outline of the plot.

———The heroine's most shocking actions come as an almost complete surprise to the other characters in the play.

———The play exploits a number of supernatural elements.
    Etc.

ATTENTION—NOTE CAREFULLY: The following questions are to be answered while you are listening to music played by the proctor of the examination. DO NOT attempt to answer them until you are instructed to do so.

Excerpts I—III will each be played in succession, once. For each item, write

  1. if the statement *best* describes Excerpt I.
  2. if the statement *best* describes Excerpt II.
  3. if the statement *best* describes Excerpt III.

———This excerpt might be the expression of basic antagonisms.

———This excerpt is related in style to Stravinsky's *The Rite of Spring.*

———This composer treats rhythm as his base and other musical elements as added adornments.

———This composer employs contrapuntal imitation in the development of his excerpt.
    Etc.

The following diagram represents, in skeleton form, the periodic table. Certain columns of the table are labeled *A, B, C,* and *D.* The letter *E* designates the location of elements of atomic numbers 88–96. For each item, write the letter indicating the location in the table to which the statement correctly refers.

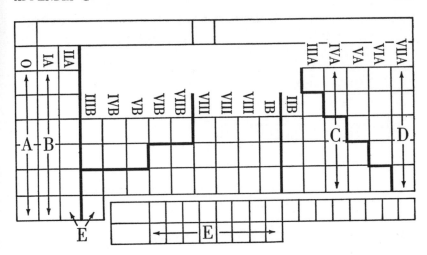

_____Elements near the top of this column share electrons when forming compounds.

_____All of the elements of this column are classified as metals.

_____The halogens are located in this column.

_____An element whose single outer electron is at the greatest distance from the nucleus of the atom is located at the bottom of this column. Etc.

Selected References

Adams, Georgia Sachs and Theodore L. Torgerson. *Measurement and Evaluation for the Secondary-School Teacher: With Implications for Corrective Procedures.* New York: Dryden Press, Inc., 1956.

Adkins, Dorothy C. *et al. Construction and Analysis of Achievement Tests.* Washington, D. C.: U. S. Civil Service Commission (Out of print), 1947.

Anastasi, Anne. *Psychological Testing.* New York: The Macmillan Co., 1954.

Army Personnel Tests and Measurement. Department of the Army Technical Manual TM12-260. Washington, D. C.: United States Government Printing Office, April, 1953.

Bean, Kenneth L. *Construction of Educational and Personnel Tests.* New York: McGraw-Hill Book Co., 1953.

Bloom, Benjamin S. (ed.). *Taxonomy of Educational Objectives: The Classification of Educational Goals: Handbook I, Cognitive Domain.* New York: Longmans, Green & Co., 1956.

Bradfield, James M. and H. Stewart Moredock. *Measurement and Evaluation in Education: An Introduction to Its Theory and Practice at Both the Elementary and Secondary School Levels.* New York: The Macmillan Co., 1957.

Buros, Oscar Krisen. *The Fifth Mental Measurements Yearbook.* Highland Park, New Jersey: The Gryphon Press, 1959.

Cronbach, Lee J. *Essentials of Psychological Testing.* New York: Harper & Bros., 1949.

Davis, Frederick B. *Item-Analysis Data: Their Computation, Interpretation, and Use in Test Construction.* Cambridge: Harvard University, Harvard Education Papers Number 2, 1946.

Dressel, Paul L. *et al. Comprehensive Examinations in a Program of General Education.* East Lansing: Michigan State University Press, 1949.

———.(ed.). *Evaluation in the Basic College at Michigan State University.* New York: Harper & Bros., 1958.

Edwards, Allen L. *Statistical Methods for the Behavioral Sciences.* New York: Rinehart & Co., 1954.

Ferguson, George A. *Statistical Analysis in Psychology and Education.* New York: McGraw-Hill Book Co., 1959.

Freeman, F. S. *Theory and Practice of Psychological Testing* (Rev. ed.). New York: Henry Holt & Co., 1955.

Garrett, Henry E. *Elementary Statistics.* New York: Longmans, Green & Co., 1956.

Gerberich, J. Raymond. *Specimen Objective Test Items: A Guide to Achievement Test Construction.* New York: Longmans, Green & Co., 1956.

Goheen, Howard W. and Samuel Kavruck. *Selected References on Test Construction, Mental Test Theory, and Statistics, 1929-1949.* Washington, D. C.: U.S. Civil Service Commission, 1950.

Goodenough, F. L. *Mental Testing.* New York: Rinehart & Co., 1949.

Green, H. A., A. N. Jorgensen, and J. R. Gerberich. *Measurement and Evaluation in the Elementary School* (2nd ed.). New York: Longmans, Green & Co., 1953.

———. *Measurement and Evaluation in the Secondary School* (2nd ed.). New York: Longmans, Green & Co., 1954.

Greene, Edward B. *Measurements of Human Behavior* (Rev. ed.). New York: The Odyssey Press, 1952.

Guilford, J. P. *Fundamental Statistics in Psychology and Education* (3rd ed.). New York: McGraw-Hill Book Co., 1956.

———. *Psychometric Methods* (2nd ed.). New York: McGraw-Hill Book Co., 1954.

Gulliksen, Harold. *Theory of Mental Tests.* New York: John Wiley & Sons, 1950.

Huff, Darrell. *How to Lie with Statistics.* New York: W. W. Norton & Co., 1954.

Jordan, A. M. *Measurement in Education: An Introduction.* New York: McGraw-Hill Book Co., 1953.

Lawshe, Charles H. Jr. *Principles of Personnel Testing.* New York: McGraw-Hill Book Co., 1948.

Lefever, D. Welty and Earl F. Carnes. *A Workbook in Measurement and Evaluation.* Los Angeles, Calif.: College Book Store, 1956.

Lindquist, E. F. (ed.). *Educational Measurement*. Washington, D. C.: American Council on Education, 1951.

McNemar, Quinn. *Psychological Statistics* (2nd ed.). New York: John Wiley & Sons, 1955.

Micheels, W. J. and M. R. Karnes. *Measuring Educational Achievement*. New York: McGraw-Hill Book Co., 1950.

Moroney, M. J. *Facts from Figures* (2nd & Rev. ed.). Baltimore, Md.: Penguin Books, Inc., 1953.

Mursell, James L. *Psychological Testing* (2nd ed.). New York: Longmans, Green & Co., 1949.

Noll, Victor H. *Introduction to Educational Measurement*. Boston, Mass.: Houghton Mifflin Co., 1957.

Odell, C. W. *How To Improve Classroom Testing* (Rev. ed). Dubuque, Iowa: Wm. C. Brown Co., 1958.

Remmers, H. H. and N. L. Gage. *Educational Measurement and Evaluation* (Rev. ed.). New York: Harper & Bros., 1955.

Ross, C. C. and J. C. Stanley. *Measurement in Today's Schools* (3rd ed.). New York: Prentice-Hall, Inc., 1954.

Stuit, Dewey. *Personnel Research and Test Development*. Princeton: Princeton University Press, 1947.

Technical Recommendations for Achievement Tests. Prepared by the Committees on Test Standards of the American Educational Research Association and the National Council on Measurements Used in Education. Washington, D.C.: American Educational Research Association, National Education Association, 1955.

Technical Recommendations for Psychological Tests and Diagnostic Techniques. Prepared by a Joint Committee of the American Psychological Association, American Educational Research Association, and National Council on Measurements Used in Education. Supplement to the *Psychological Bulletin*, Vol. 51, No. 2, Part 2, March, 1954.

Thomas, R. M. *Judging Student Progress*. New York: Longmans, Green & Co., 1954.

Thorndike, Robert L. *Personnel Selection: Test and Measurement Techniques*. New York: John Wiley & Sons, 1949.

Thorndike, Robert L. and Elizabeth Hagen. *Measurement and Evaluation in Psychology and Education*. New York: John Wiley & Sons, 1955.

Travers, R. M. W. *Educational Measurement*. New York: The Macmillan Co., 1955.

———. *How To Make Achievement Tests.* New York: The Odyssey Press, 1950.

Traxler, Arthur E., Robert Jacobs, Margaret Selover, and Agatha Townsend. *Introduction to Testing and the Use of Test Results in Public Schools.* New York: Harper & Bros., 1953.

Vernon, Philip E. *The Measurement of Abilities* (2nd ed.). London: University of London Press Ltd., 1956.

Index of Names

Index of Subjects